# Foundations of an Elite Culture

# Foundations of an Elite Culture

## Building Success with High Standards and a Positive Environment

David Arencibia

ConnectEDD Publishing
Hanover, Pennsylvania

This publication is available at discount pricing when purchased in quantity for educational purposes, promotions, or fundraisers. For inquiries and details, contact the publisher at: info@connecteddpublishing.com

Published by ConnectEDD Publishing LLC
Hanover, PA
www.connecteddpublishing.com

Cover Design: Kheila Casas

Foundations of an Elite Culture by David Arencibia. —1st ed. Paperback
ISBN 979-8-9890027-2-6

# ConnectEDD
## PUBLISHING

# Praise for *Foundations of an Elite Culture*

Dr. David Arencibia has written a must-read for anyone committed to building a school culture that is rooted in high standards and a positive environment. This book is filled with practical application and turn-key strategies that your school can use right away. If you are looking for a book that helps build momentum in your school, *Foundations of an Elite Culture* is a must-read for educators.

—Jon Gordon | 16x bestselling author; author of *The Energy Bus*

*Foundations of an Elite Culture* contains powerful real-life stories and case studies, providing a comprehensive blueprint for building a thriving school culture. This definitive guide offers invaluable resources for schools and principals seeking direction. With its thorough coverage of every aspect of school life and thought-provoking guiding questions, it keeps readers on track. By the final page, you'll emerge equipped with the precise tools and insights needed to cultivate an elite culture within your school community.

—Dr. Jim Van Allan | bestselling author of *The Energy Bus for Schools*

In *Foundations of an Elite Culture*, David Arencibia provides a robust framework for leaders wanting to take their schools to the next level. From passionate stories from the field to research-proven strategies to implement now, this book is one that I wish I had at the beginning of my principalship.

—Beth Houf | Author of Lead Like a PIRATE, 2022 National Principal of the Year, 2021 Missouri Principal of the Year, and High School Principal

What a fantastic resource for leaders! Whether you're new to a school and building culture for the first time or a veteran leader who needs to refresh the organization, all leaders can find what they need in *Foundations of an Elite Culture*. Packed with core strategies, the author leads principals to reflect on their own practice and then interweaves his own personal account of struggle and challenge on his journey to become a nationally recognized leader. I found myself building my next year's "to do" list with intentionality as I read this book. David Arencibia leaves nothing out—from hiring, to developing and implementing core values, to effectively leveraging the strengths of every individual on the team. In these pages, it's easy to appreciate how employing the strategies that David describes slowly but certainly builds momentum toward reaching a strong, self-sustaining, winning school culture where "hope takes root."

—Donna Hayward | 2023 National Principal of the Year, 2022
　　Connecticut Principal of the Year, and High School Principal

David's *Elite Culture* is a masterclass in educational leadership, offering a step-by-step guide to forging strong relationships and an elite school culture. The book serves as the ultimate playbook for transforming any educational environment, offering a detailed blueprint comprising his proven strategies. It's a practical, insightful resource that promises real transformation. This book is an essential read for educators committed to excellence.

—Chris Layton | CharacterStrong Executive Director of National
　　Development

Dr. David Arencibia has captured the essence of building an elite school culture through the principles of high standards and a positive environment. His personal story is captivating as he shares the building blocks that influenced his life and personal development. This is a must-read book for educators, business leaders, and those who wish to make a difference.

—Archie McAfee | Executive Director of the Texas Association of Secondary School Principals (TASSP)

Dr. David Arencibia's *Foundations of an Elite Culture* is a true gem for educators ready to take their practice to the next level. This book masterfully illustrates the integration of high standards with a positive environment, offering invaluable insights for creating a culture of excellence that everyone craves. With its wealth of practical tools and real-world examples, this book is a beacon of inspiration, guiding educators toward success in both the classroom and beyond. The level of engagement pouring out of each page is precisely what education needs today!

—Jonathan Alsheimer | bestselling author of *Next Level Teaching*, Keynote Speaker, and Teacher

*Foundations of an Elite Culture* is a well planned and executed road map for ANYONE seeking to gain substantial knowledge and education on building an *Elite* foundation to become successful in any area of your life. Being a former professional athlete, I wish I had a blueprint like this one when I was coming up through high school to college! Serious gems and building blocks littered throughout the reading!

—Ron Brooks | Veteran Collegiate and NFL Football Player for the Philadelphia Eagles and Buffalo Bills

Dr. Arencibia has masterfully created a winning formula for building elite culture by building an elite team of elite team members. Through the power of self-discovery and strengths finding, organizations can create workplace engines powered by teams who are motivated to win. Dr. Arencibia has successfully demonstrated how re-engineering an elite culture starts with developing leaders from the inside out and creating a triumphant atmosphere where every person is an all-star. Leaders now have a blueprint to create their own dream team of elite performers while normalizing a cycle of winning that is relentlessly positive and audaciously irresistible.

—Dr. Brian L. Matthews | ACUE Tenured Associate Professor of Management, Texas A&M University-Texarkana

Dr. David Arencibia's *Foundations of an Elite Culture* is a must-read for every campus leader. This insightful book offers a comprehensive guide to building a culture of excellence in education, addressing key areas such as cultivating a positive environment, defining mission and values, celebrating achievements, and preventing burnout. It's an indispensable resource for leaders dedicated to transforming their campuses into thriving hubs of learning and growth.

—Rick Westfall | Retired Public Education Superintendent

Dr. David Arencibia's book, *Foundations of an Elite Culture*, is exactly what our educational world needs right now. I've had the privilege of knowing David for nearly a decade and have seen these strategies firsthand in action. David's leadership exemplifies authenticity, and the book brings this ethos to life. *Elite Culture* showcases the transformative power of fostering a positive and inclusive school environment, emphasizing the direct link between educators' and students' well-being and success. Through his insightful guidance, David demonstrates how to cultivate a culture where everyone feels valued and empowered to thrive. His dedication to illustrating how to shape a positive school culture is truly commendable, making this book a valuable resource for educators and leaders alike.

—Michele McWilliams | Gallup Strengths Certified Coach, and 2015 Arkansas Principal of the Year

Dr. David Arencibia's *Foundations of an Elite Culture: Building Success with High Standards and a Positive Environment* delivers the strategies, examples, and messages we all need to provide staff members, students, parents, and community members an appreciative, positive, and safe campus to collaborative with enthusiasm and productively support all stakeholders. Dr. Arencibia delivers the message on the importance of creating unforgettable moments for all involved, resulting in excitement in being at the workplace and in the classroom.

—Adam Lane | 2022 Florida Principal of the Year, and K-12 Dive
2022 National Principal of the Year, and Principal

Dr. David Arencibia's *Foundations of an Elite Culture* is a transformative read that seamlessly bridges the gap between lofty ideals and practical application. This book provides educators, leaders, and visionaries with a robust framework to elevate their environments across all professional spectrums. Dr. Arencibia's rich narrative, combined with vivid stories and actionable strategies, invites readers to embrace high standards and positivity, promising to shift paradigms and catalyze genuine progress. Whether you are steering a classroom or a new or seasoned leader, this book delivers essential tools and inspiration to create an elite culture that fosters a culture of excellence that empowers individuals and teams—a must-read for those dedicated to cultivating an environment of success and positivity.

—Jana Clark | 2023 Texas Assistant Principal of the Year, and
Elementary School Principal

In *Foundations of an Elite Culture*, David Arencibia has masterfully articulated a recipe for success. I have witnessed first-hand these strategies at work. He is a high-functioning, intelligent person who has crafted a formula for building an elite culture in a common sense and practical way. David uses his unique ability to apply equal heavy hands of high standards and a positive environment to create the perfect foundation for elite culture, and we get to be a part of that journey.

—Mark Smith | Head Football Coach/Athletic Coordinator at San Angelo Central HS in San Angelo ISD, Former coach at the Universities of Oklahoma, Colorado, Arkansas, and SMU

Dr. Arencibia's message in *Foundations of an Elite Culture*, is both relatable and relevant for today's leaders. This book provides the necessary focus on building organizational capacity that leads to a positive climate and a culture of high expectations.

—Conrad Streeter | Deputy Superintendent, Hurst-Euless-Bedford ISD

# DEDICATION

I dedicate this book to all educators and leaders who impact our current and future generations daily. Your dedication and guidance are invaluable. Thank you to those who exemplify effective leadership and have shaped my understanding of leadership. Your influence inspires me to be a better leader each day.

This dedication is for readers who embrace a growth mindset and strive to create a better world, whether personally or professionally. Thank you for your willingness to be molded and positively influenced.

Together, let us continue to invest in building a better and more positive world.

# Table of Contents

# Introduction

This book aims to provide practical strategies and tools for creating a highly effective, engaging, and positive culture in the classroom, school, team, workplace, and many other settings. While the book's background and expertise are firmly rooted in education, many leadership attributes, lessons, and principles broadly apply to many other life or professional settings. It emphasizes the importance of balancing high standards and a positive environment and how combining these two crucial elements fosters a culture of excellence. Specifically, an *Elite Culture*. An elite culture embodies the fusion of high standards and a positive environment, creating a dynamic synergy that nurtures the highest level of culture possible.

To build the two pillars of an elite culture, one must possess the necessary ingredients and materials, including a clear and concise mission that speaks to the "why" of the organization. One must also have a deep understanding of one's own strengths and talents, as well as the strengths of those around them. Additionally, a commitment to specific core values that serve as guiding principles and actionable items is essential for propelling the journey forward and creating a thriving culture.

For educators, this book serves as a compelling reminder of the transformative power that individuals and education can have on today's generation, completely altering a student's trajectory for the better and propelling students, staff, teams, schools, and communities toward excellence. In today's post-pandemic world, characterized by a workforce shortage, there is a pressing need to cultivate environments in which talent is inclined to stay, fostering positive work settings and enabling entities to retain their employees. Employing the proven strategies from the Elite Culture framework will help prevent burnout and cultivate high employee engagement. The impact of these strategies will have a direct effect on overall student engagement, well-being, attendance, and academic success. Educators will also find new ways to cultivate a thriving and engaged culture of success. This book contains embedded QR codes designed to enhance the examples and strategies presented, offering visual illustrations to bring the printed word to life. For those outside of education, this book will help galvanize the understanding behind the need to create environments in which you and those around you can thrive at home, work, and in life.

This book urges readers to take charge of their environment, emphasizing high standards and positivity to empower others and create a ripple effect of excellence. My hope is that anyone reading this book will glean practical strategies and tools for fostering a highly effective, engaging, and positive environment. As you read the following pages, you'll understand the essence of an Elite Culture, emphasizing the fusion of high standards and a positive environment to propel individuals, teams, schools, and organizations toward excellence.

# CHAPTER 1

~

# Elite Culture

## Navigating Life and Creating an Elite Culture: Davey's Story

Life is a journey filled with obstacles, challenges, and unexpected turns. How we respond to these events shapes who we are and influences the environments we create. Davey's life journey has been filled with obstacles, but he has never let those challenges define him. His early life included a brief period of homelessness, financial hardship growing up in situational poverty, learning disabilities, and some societal rejection due to his socioeconomic status.

Imagine a child growing up in the lowest financial percentile in the country, mired in poverty, at times navigating gang-ridden streets, and contending with an undiagnosed learning disability that became a barrier to overcome in his schooling. Davey's father's family moved from Cuba in the 1950s to escape the grips of Fidel Castro's aggressive communist regime. His father reached the 9th grade. Davey's mother was raised in a middle-class Mexican family before moving to America as a teenager, achieving an 8th-grade education. Davey's parents relentlessly loved both their sons and did everything possible for them as best as they knew how.

Not many would have thought that Davey, who stood in line with his mom to receive a box of free government cheese his 5th grade school year, would one day achieve success and wield power to positively influence numerous lives. It sounded impossible–or, at best, far-fetched. The challenges were substantial, including periods of a transient lifestyle with frequent relocations, creating instability. During his kindergarten through 9th-grade school years, Davey attended eight different schools. He grappled with dyslexia and ADHD, which made school particularly tough at times. During his elementary school years, dyslexia wasn't as recognized or accommodated in schools as it is today. His environment was often turbulent, exposing him to daily violence. In third grade, he walked nearly a mile to school through graffiti-infested streets and alleyways, facing an almost daily threat of being jumped by a local gang of teenagers and young adults in their early 20s because he would wear a red hand-me-down sweatshirt to keep warm during the cold northern California mornings. Red was the rival gang's color. Faced with two options, he could either walk a longer distance to school, opting for a different route, or he could remove his red sweatshirt and walk, sometimes sprinting past the gang members in order to avoid a potential daily beating.

It was around that same period in his life that tragedy occurred in a similar alleyway–his older brother's close friend from middle school was fatally shot with a 12-gauge shotgun for being in the wrong place at the wrong time. Davey would vividly remember his brother's traumatized state, leading him to stay home from school, mourning the loss of his friend. These early life experiences instilled in him the realization of life's brevity and fragility. He would later see one of his teenage friends become incarcerated for attempted murder. From a young age, he understood life was precious, and he needed to maximize opportunities to their fullest potential despite the cards he was dealt. Coupled with the deep faith rooted in Davey by his mom and a relentless pursuit of faith in God, these pivotal moments reinforced his belief that challenges were relative and perspective was key. If Davey wasn't facing life-or-death situations, he knew he would be OK. Perspective became one of his guiding principles.

Such a child might seem destined to face a tough life or even become a negative statistic in our society due to the challenging environments around him. Despite some of his surroundings, he unknowingly assumed leadership roles in the streets where he played ball or on the playgrounds at school. By other people's standards, he didn't fit the typical leader profile based on his background. Still, his life experiences made him a unique leader with unconventional approaches because of his perspective. He wasn't accustomed to a "normal" environment, as most others around him experienced, so he made sense of the world as he knew it. He discovered that it benefited him to have a positive mindset, which he learned from watching others respond to their hardships and trauma. He learned from resilient individuals how to overcome life's setbacks, realizing that negative responses to challenges hindered success. Recognizing that positive and negative reactions yield consequences, he adopted a mindset of focusing on controllable aspects, keeping life on track positively. Life is relative to each individual. Simply focus on what you can control, and don't let the things you can't control negatively affect you.

Like anyone in this world, Davey couldn't achieve anything alone. He had a loving family and mentors around him, including teachers like Mr. Conrad, who took the time to teach him chess—a passion of his teacher that inspired Davey. This mentorship motivated Davey to stay after school to be a part of the chess club and learn how to play from Mr. Conrad—even though it meant taking the only bus provided by the school for all after-school activities and tutorials for the entire student body. Davey spent nearly an hour and a half on the school bus, watching other students disembark at their stops. After being dropped off at his bus stop, he walked home in the dark, reaching there many hours after the last school bell had already rung.

Mr. Conrad taught Davey the game of chess while inadvertently imparting the value of mentorship and the impact it could have on a person's life. Investing time and his passion into his students sparked a passion within Davey to love and value his teachers' passion. That's the impact an individual can have on another when sharing their passions in life.

Davey embraced the positive environment created by his teacher, focusing on becoming the best chess player possible at his age and winning his all-school chess tournament. One of Davey's learning disabilities would become a strength. Sometimes, individuals with dyslexia will have higher visual-spatial skills, allowing them to be creative and visually see things differently than others. A perceived weakness became a strength. He would absorb the nuances of high-level play from Mr. Conrad, who had experience competing in world tournaments against some of the best chess players in the world. Through this mentorship, Mr. Conrad inadvertently instilled a valuable lesson in Davey. He demonstrated that success was attainable by cultivating a positive environment. This environment was fueled with passion and with the highest standards of learning. Davey didn't mind the extra time spent at school or the long commute home because he was invested in the elite environment that Mr. Conrad had created—a setting with high standards in the game, coupled with a positive environment fostered through his investment of time into his students and his love and passion for the game.

Investing time and his passion into his students sparked a passion within Davey to love and value his teachers' passion. That's the impact an individual can have on another when sharing their passions in life.

Like Davey, everyone has their own unique stories, along with individual strengths and talents. We all aspire to be part of an environment of positivity, willing to put in the hard work that comes with high expectations, as long as that environment aligns with our passion and is a place where we feel valued. Regardless of the setting, we all appreciate recognition for the work we do; we share a common desire to feel appreciated. In some aspect of life, work, or home, we aspire to be part of an elite culture that pushes us to be our best in whatever aspect we choose to focus our time and attention. Yet, we acknowledge that burnout is likely without a positive environment that connects with us, encouraging, motivating, and celebrating the good things happening around us.

The reason I am personally passionate about guiding others to create an elite environment is because I am Davey. Adversity and challenges have helped cultivate my mindset. Despite everyday challenges, I have learned that one can choose their response to their circumstances. By focusing on controllable aspects and maintaining a positive outlook, I can focus on things within my control. Mentorship plays a crucial role in shaping individuals, particularly through the guidance of positive mentors like my teacher, Mr. Conrad. Where would I be without the heroes around me who mentored, taught, and helped instill a positive mindset to overcome life's inevitable challenges? My life would have turned out very differently. That's why I am passionate about sharing stories and strategies to help guide others today on what is already inside them—the desire to have love and joy in life, manifested in whatever we choose to focus our time and attention. It is why my mission is to help others create environments of excellence.

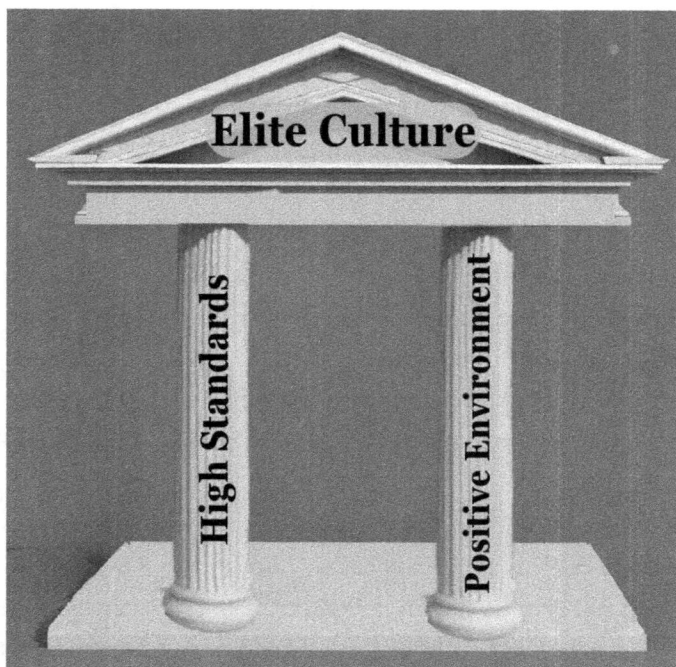

## Objectives For an Elite Culture: Building the Foundational Pillars with 7 Key Concepts

Like any seasoned teacher, quickly laying out objectives is crucial. This book explores proven leadership strategies derived from best practices in various settings. Key concepts and stories are illustrated with examples from elite cultures. Together, we will build the foundation for an *Elite Culture* on two critical pillars:

**Pillar 1: High Standards**
**Pillar 2: Positive Environment**

# ELITE CULTURE

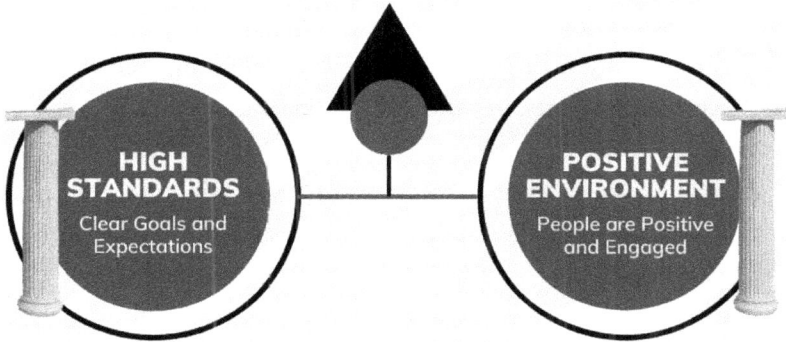

We will look at what it takes to create these two pillars, breaking down the key ingredients for constructing the pillars, which include:

A. **Elite Mission:** There's always a clear focus on the end goal.
B. **Elite Values:** Your values align with how you want to accomplish your mission.

The fibers of the materials within the pillars include the following:

1. **Elite Strengths** Understanding how to utilize our own personal strengths and talents, as well as those of the people around us, is crucial for maximizing potential and achieving success.
2. **Elite Team** Building a team that aligns with our core values helps to execute our mission effectively.

FOUNDATIONS OF AN ELITE CULTURE

3. **Elite Awareness (Preventing Burnout and Retaining Talent)** A deep understanding of why one chooses to do the work and comprehending what motivates them and you to excel fosters a sense of connection.
4. **Elite Momentum** We create momentum by celebrating all accomplishments, big and small, and by avoiding always working in silos.
5. **Elite Celebration** Raise the praise! We celebrate everything, fostering a collective uplifting that propels the momentum forward for everyone on the team.
6. **Elite Community** Engage the entire school [or workplace] community; it takes a village.
7. **Elite Engagement** Engagement vs. Compliance: there's a difference.

When we comprehend our unique strengths and talents, we can more positively impact others. When we truly understand and use our strengths, we shine like no one else because these strengths and skills, when combined, are uniquely our own, and no one else in this world can duplicate them. There is only one you—which makes you unique. By recognizing your strengths and understanding how they contribute to your purpose and mission, we benefit from our work and enhance the well-being of those around us—our team.

No one succeeds alone, and we all need the support and encouragement of others to reach our fullest potential. Through our daily interactions, we contribute to shaping our current and future generations, embodying why we serve as educators, colleagues, leaders, and mentors. While this responsibility is great, this book is filled with strategies designed to alleviate the burden on our shoulders and enable us to concentrate on the crucial work of being the best for those around us. Creating engaging environments with a positive outlook is the essence of the work. In today's society, grit and determination can take us a long way individually. Still, how we interact and work with others elevates our ceiling and leadership capacity. Together, we can initiate a ripple effect of positivity and growth that extends far beyond ourselves.

The world is constantly evolving, especially following the COVID-19 pandemic. People everywhere are starving for individuals to take positive action to make our world a better place. This task is challenging, but essential, for reaching our full potential. We need influential leaders now more than ever in education and all other professions. Leaders can help navigate troubled waters and become a beacon of hope and change to counter the negative narrative. Simply put, we need positive change to transform outdated practices into best practices in many professions, including education. Different thinking is essential to getting different–and better–results.

This book will discuss the problems facing education in a post-COVID world. These include the general workforce shortage, which includes educators, the need for teacher retention, and how we can create innovative and engaging learning environments.

We know that the environment we create significantly impacts everyone around us. How do we strike a balance between maintaining high standards for success and fostering a culture of positivity? We will unlock the tools to achieve this balance and create an environment in which staff and students are excited to participate each day.

We will evaluate the importance of a pillar of high standards (pillar 1) and how it can motivate and inspire while exploring the value of a second pillar of a positive environment (pillar 2) and its impact on engagement, mental health, and well-being. We will explore this by looking at high-performing educational environments that formed dynamic teams, including teachers, coaches, mentors, support staff, volunteers, and the school community. Additionally, we'll examine other elite examples in various professions, such as the service industry.

We will also look at strategies that involve establishing and embodying core values to enhance the overall culture of a school and its programs. These strategies have garnered attention from various publications, such as Education Week and NASSP's Principal Leadership Magazine, some leading sources for professional development in education. The proven strategies have also received recognition from influential leaders and programs, such as CharacterStrong, the National Association of Secondary School Principals, multiple universities, and the bestselling book, *The Energy Bus for Schools* by authors Jon Gordon and Dr. Jim Van Allan.

Ultimately, this book will offer leadership lessons and strategies for merging the two pillars of high standards and a positive environment to establish a solid foundation for an elite culture. This book isn't just a collection of ideas—it's a call to action. It's time to create an elite culture of excellence where everyone can thrive and succeed at the highest levels. Let's go!

CHAPTER 2

~

# Elite Pillars
## *High Standards and Positive Environment*

## The Balance Between the Power of High Standards and a Positive Environment

Most people dream of being part of a high-performing organization with a positive environment. When these two pillars are combined, they create a culture of excellence that paves the way for remarkable success.

Many organizations excel in only one of the foundational pillars of an elite culture. Some prioritize high standards, emphasizing structured, efficient, data-driven systems and accountability while neglecting positive environment. Others solely focus on cultivating relationships, overlooking productivity elements. When only focusing on high standards, there is a strong emphasis on a business-only focused approach, leaving individuals yearning for a more relational side because people and their feelings towards their environment matter, especially in education or service-oriented professions.

Conversely, environments focused solely on harmony and avoiding conflict often lack growth and accountability, hindering the ability to achieve exceptional results. This fear of crucial conversations may impede progress.

This brings us to the central challenge: where should the focus lie? Should it be about maintaining high standards of expectation or creating a positive environment? Simply put, elite cultures excel at both. They skillfully balance a relentless focus on cultivating a positive environment while setting high expectations. Balancing these two concepts is the key to transitioning from a good to a remarkable entity, ultimately leading to an elite culture over time.

This transformation requires attention to detail and unwavering determination, each directed towards these crucial concepts. The more intricate the attention to detail and the stronger the determination towards each idea, the more profound your journey towards an excellent environment will be. Elite cultures stand out by excelling in high standards and positive environment, emphasizing a strong focus on each aspect. That's the magic that an elite culture brings to the table.

## One Step at a Time

Everything worth doing takes time, so take it one step at a time. These shared ideas, events, and strategies will take time. There are no shortcuts to creating environments of excellence. The ideas may feel overwhelming if none are already in place. Allow yourself to tackle the giant elephant of creating an elite culture one bite at a time. You are already on the right path and should be commended as long as you've committed to the journey. Like anything else done at a high level, investing daily, weekly, monthly, and annual year-after-year time and effort is a requirement. Choose one thing and focus on how to develop it over time. Then, choose the next thing when the first becomes part of the regular day-to-day routine, and so on. I will repeat this later to remind you that creating this environment is a marathon, not a sprint.

## Why an Elite Culture? Insights from an Elite Coach

Why focus on creating an elite culture? Simply put, anything worthy of the relentless investment of your time and attention should enable you to reach the highest levels of excellence in whatever you pursue.

There has been a recent wave of significant retirements by some of the most elite football coaches in both the National Football League (NFL) and among major Division 1 College Football programs. Bill Belichick is often hailed as one of the greatest head coaches in NFL history. He notably holds the record for the most Super Bowl wins as a head coach, securing six championships. His combined Super Bowl victories as coach and coordinator are eight, marking the highest total in NFL Super Bowl history.

One of Bill Belichick's understudies was Nick Saban, considered one of the greatest Division 1 college football coaches ever. Saban boasted an impressive .877% winning record and has secured seven national titles as a head coach, the most in college football history. Both coaches reached the most elite levels in their profession.

During one of Coach Saban's many memorable press conferences, he discussed having five choices in life regarding our professions, including choosing to become "elite." Here's the transcript:

"You know, we actually have about five choices in our life. We can be bad at what we do. We can be average at what we do. I mean, we can be good at what we do—which is probably God's expectation for whatever ability he gave us. Or we can be excellent...or we can be elite."

Everybody has a choice as to what they want to do and how they want to do that. But if you're going to be excellent or elite, you've got to do special things. You have to have special intentions, you have to have a special focus, you have to have a special commitment, drive, and passion to do things at a high level and a high standard all of the time.

It doesn't matter what God given ability that you have...that probably can make you good. But without the rest of it, I'm not sure if you ever get excellent or elite, and that's the part that we're trying to get to."

Saban, N. (2019, April 7). Press conference discussion on the five choices in life. [Transcript of press conference].

When creating this book, I knew that, like anything else, the examples, strategies, and leadership philosophies would resonate with many. I chose to focus on some examples and techniques that would help set individuals apart from others. At the end of the day, you are investing your time to become better, grow, and improve; why not have goals, events, processes, and moments at the elite level? Our time and energy are worth it. Our passions, strengths, and focus deserve it. Like any worthwhile goal, by creating an elite culture, we will find success regardless of where we may land at the end of our journey. Like the expression by Norman Vincent Peale, best-selling author of *The Power of Positive Thinking*, he said: "Shoot for the moon. Even if you miss, you'll land among the stars." (Peale, 1952)

In light of these considerations, and with a proven track record of achieving the highest levels of success, Coach Saban understood that attaining elite status demands a particular type of focus. Coach Saban and Coach Belichick profoundly grasped the prerequisites for being elite, specifically emphasizing Pillar 1—maintaining high standards— surpassing all expectations. Let's look at the first pillar of having high standards.

## High Standards: (Pillar 1)

High standards form one of the two foundational pillars for creating a thriving environment, providing a solid framework for achievement. They are part of the foundation that holds up any thriving entity, driving individuals to strive for excellence. Whether it's a school or a company committed to delivering top-notch products and services, high standards set these entities apart from their competitors. Establishing a culture of high standards necessitates an unwavering pursuit of excellence in all aspects of the organization.

Make no mistake: your school, business, team, and entity have a primary purpose–your ultimate mission. During his tenure as an elite coach, Coach Saban was known for a quote that encapsulated the process and the foundation of Pillar One–high standards. He would often say, "Don't worry about winning. Just focus on doing your job at the highest level for every single play, and the wins will follow." (Pep Unlimited, 2022)

Simply put, concentrate on the details of the task at hand to achieve the best possible outcome. What is it that you are trying to accomplish? This simple question should guide you toward reaching your success. Take a moment to think about the ultimate mission that you, personally or professionally, are on. Whatever that clear mission is, your standards, expectations, and everything you do in the bulk of your day should be focused on that goal.

Here are some major themes within the pillar of high standards that we will cover throughout the book:

1.  **Clear Vision and Mission:** Define your goals clearly and have a mission for executing them.
2.  **Highest Attainable Goals:** Set ambitious, achievable goals to maintain focus.
3.  **Be Your Best:** Pay attention to detail and give your best effort.
4.  **Data-Driven Approach:** Use data to track progress and identify areas for improvement.
5.  **Engaging Environment:** Foster engagement and meaning in the work process for yourself and those around you.

**HIGH STANDARDS**

1 VISION & MISSION
Work towards a mission daily

2 HIGHEST GOALS POSSIBLE
Highest achievable goals. Set obtainable goals along the way.

3 BE YOUR BEST
Best effort by each individual and whole team daily.

4 DATA DRIVEN
Review all data available and improve. Refine your systems and processes.

5 ENGAGING ENVIRONMENT
Maximizing time. Engagement vs. Compliance

HIGH STANDARDS
Expectations. Goals. Non-Negotiables.

# Positive Environment: (Pillar 2)

While high standards are critical, they are not enough to create an elite culture, especially in today's society. A positive environment is essential for sustained success in a service-setting industry like education. Positive relationships contribute to morale and cultivate an engaging environment, encouraging employees to do their best. In an environment where individuals feel supported and valued, they are more likely to take risks and push themselves outside their comfort zone. A positive environment fosters a sense of belonging and encourages individuals to work collaboratively towards a common goal.

Many environments can be mundane. If you're lucky, you might encounter a basic greeting, a straightforward task to be completed, and an overall OK experience when you enter such places. You simply go in, do what needs to be done, and move on to the next thing. The task is accomplished, and everything seems fine, but nothing is exceptional about the environment or experience.

Now, imagine a different kind of place. A place where you can sense a palpable shift in the atmosphere as soon as you step into it. It's a space where a strong sense of community prevails, where people greet you with smiles and a friendly demeanor. A positive atmosphere thrives in this environment, which you can feel and observe. You find yourself drawn to this place, wanting to be a part of it. The task you went there to accomplish takes on a new dimension. Being in that environment is enjoyable, and you don't mind spending time there because of the positive atmosphere. Whether in school, business or within a team, it becomes a place where you want to be, where you feel inspired to do your best and be your best.

To reiterate, it's not just about fulfilling a task; it's about experiencing a profound difference in how you feel. You genuinely desire to be present in that environment because of the positive energy it exudes. It creates a sense of belonging and transforms day-to-day tasks into meaningful experiences. This distinction highlights the power of a positive environment and its impact on individuals and their well-being.

Here are some major themes within the pillar of positive environment that we will cover and gain strategies throughout the book:

1. **Relationships:** It's all about the people. Relationships matter. Get to know one another; an investment in the people is an investment in the culture.
2. **Family Atmosphere:** Create that atmosphere wherever and whenever you can to help make the environment familiar and conducive to the required work.
3. **Positivity:** Lead with positive intent. Create a welcoming environment where people can thrive.
4. **Team:** We are not in this alone. Two is better than one, and three is better than two. Come together as individuals with unique strengths and be united to form an elite team.
5. **Celebrate:** Celebrate everything. It helps inspire and builds momentum to continue the work being done.

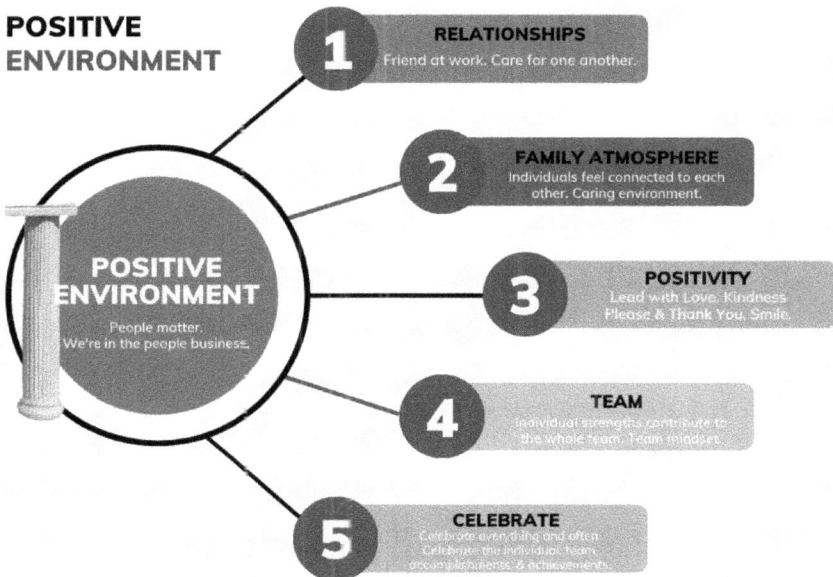

**POSITIVE ENVIRONMENT**

**POSITIVE ENVIRONMENT**
People matter. We're in the people business.

**1 RELATIONSHIPS**
Friend at work. Care for one another.

**2 FAMILY ATMOSPHERE**
Individuals feel connected to each other. Caring environment.

**3 POSITIVITY**
Lead with Love. Kindness. Please & Thank You. Smile.

**4 TEAM**
Individual strengths contribute to the whole team. Team mindset.

**5 CELEBRATE**
Celebrate everything and often. Celebrate the individual, team, accomplishments & achievements.

## Pillar 1 (High Standards) without Pillar 2 (Positive Environment)

It is critical to acknowledge that today's society has undergone significant changes, especially after the COVID-19 period. Those who have experienced a time when the daily grind and the prospect of feeling "fine" regularly were accepted norms must recognize that such experiences are no longer desired or widely shared in today's society. That's why an environment that focuses only on high standards is typically not sustainable for its people. Having high standards and expectations without the human relations side can create a sense of monotony, an unfulfilling feeling of a daily grind with no positives to accompany it, burnout, and sometimes a sense of having no purpose.

## Cracks in the Pillar: Blake's Story

It feels like yesterday when I recall speaking with Blake, a teacher who had experienced significant success in pushing students to excel in math. Students perceived Blake as a good teacher because of their class performance, but there was a lack of close teacher-student relationships. While students were progressing, the environment felt somewhat cold and overly task-driven, lacking relational connection experiences.

Blake became frustrated with the diminishing determination and self-motivation seen in students compared to previous years. He had been accustomed to an environment in which students were more compliant when he began as a teacher nearly a decade earlier.

After the pandemic struck, Blake noticed a significant decline in students' focus on their studies and academic gaps created by the shift away from in-person instruction, a trend now extensively documented in educational research. Bewildered as a teacher-leader, Blake eventually chose to leave the profession.

One thing Blake lacked was having connections—not only with students, but also with colleagues. In a way, he felt isolated and alone, leading to the difficult decision to leave the education profession. Blake would later tell me he yearned for a different time, when classes were filled with compliant students ready to sit, listen, and learn, intrinsically dedicated to their studies.

Blake was accustomed to having a foundational pillar of high standards in the classroom and performance, without emphasizing the importance of a positive relational culture. I wonder if he had built more relationships with students and colleagues, would that have helped him hang on a few more years in the profession? Could allocating precious time at his door, greeting students, or incorporating connection pieces in warm-ups or exit tickets with students build community? Would giving a brief break away from what would be described as relentless math-only bell-to-bell work have created stability and understanding with the students, fostering a space for them to do more when asked for it?

Building relationships upfront allows for faster progress in the work later while maintaining high standards throughout the school year. The expression "You have to go slow to go fast" applies here. I believe that it would have made a difference. Blake's story is one of many rooted primarily in the pillar of high standards. When relying solely on one foundational pillar, as Blake did, cracks may appear during societal changes or academic restrictions, such as in-person learning challenges from COVID-19 or a shift in a student's individual determination. These factors can cause the structure to crack, break, and fall when standing alone.

Now, let's look at pillar two and what can happen when it tries to stand alone.

## Pillar 2 (Positive Environment) without Pillar 1 (High Standards)

When the sole focus is on people and their feelings and maintaining a harmonious atmosphere without aligning it with high standards, the quality of the end goals can suffer. If the primary concern becomes avoiding confrontation or discomfort, the work may suffer as critical issues go unaddressed. Crucial conversations are compromised or non-existent, creating a stagnant environment with little growth.

When the sole focus is on the relational side of the individual and catering to only their emotional needs rather than considering the mission, collective goals, and outcomes of the shared entity, such as a school, team, or business, the overall quality of the work can be compromised. To achieve optimal results, it is essential to maintain a holistic approach that values both the individual and the collective objectives. Remember, your work has an underlying goal that should be achieved.

## Leadership Lid: The Impact of Only Prioritizing Relational Environment over High Standards

To illustrate the "Leadership Lid" and the impact of prioritizing relational culture over high standards, let's say we have an educator named Samantha. Samantha has held various educational positions for over two decades. While serving in the HR department, Samantha played a crucial role in hiring the school district's workforce. Although a competent educator and a good leader, Samantha maintained the norm set by predecessors, placing primary importance on relational aspects with colleagues. Samantha prioritized being nice and friendly and identified individuals who would not "rock the boat" when attracting future employees, including campus and district-level leaders.

The emphasis on an individual's character was crucial to Samantha, which is essential; however, it often overshadowed the proven or unproven track record of success of the candidates. Despite the significance of personal characteristics in the service industry, especially in education, Samantha overlooked the characteristics of Pillar 1—having high standards. This led to a restriction on the caliber of leadership the school district attracted, as the emphasis was primarily on relational aspects and behind-the-scenes politics, diminishing the significance of Pillar 1's results-driven approach with high standards. As John Maxwell (1998) discusses in *The 21 Irrefutable Laws of Leadership*, specifically regarding the "Law of the Lid." Samantha's ability to recruit elite leaders was limited due to her emphasis on relational qualities. This, in turn, affected the schools, bringing in new leaders who were typically average and unlikely to elevate the school or department to the highest levels possible. Due to such hiring practices, other school districts and professional organizations often recruited elite leaders away from Samantha's school district. Samantha's role and influence on leadership in making the final decisions on hiring major hires was significant. The impact of these practices was well-documented, and the results of the individuals hired became immediately transparent to various school communities. High-level educators chose to leave a well-established district and schools, often pointing to ineffective leadership as their reason for leaving.

Examples like that are why it is essential to recognize that being an elite leader in any role requires a balanced focus on both Pillar 1—high standards—and Pillar 2—a positive environment. Emphasizing one over the other limits the ability to achieve true elite excellence in a profession and caps one's leadership level.

## The Elite Combination

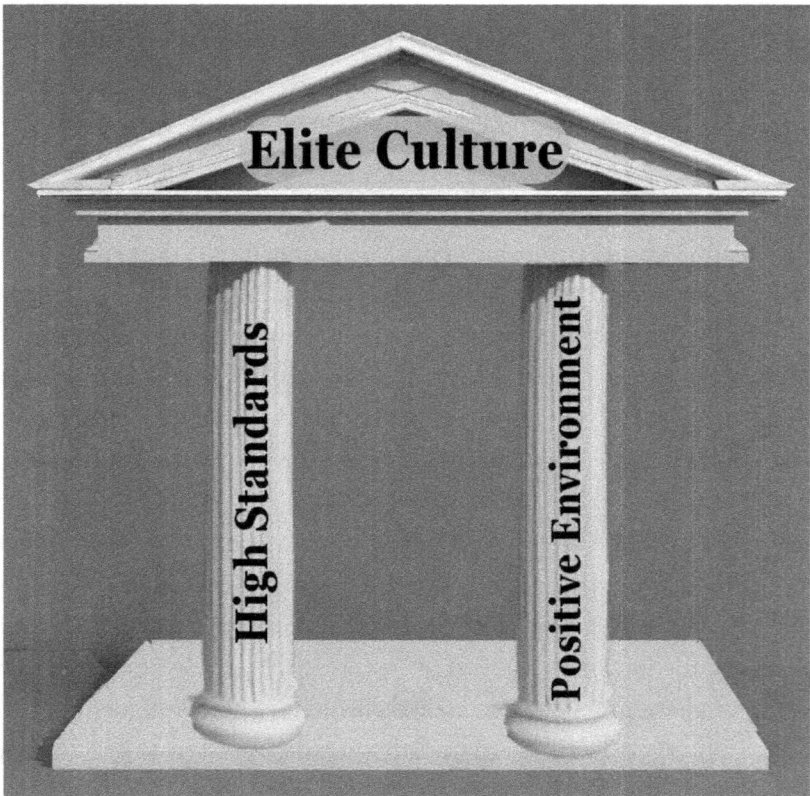

Successful organizations have both high standards and a positive environment. This combination creates a culture of excellence, an elite culture that leads to high levels of success. Individuals are challenged to perform at their best while feeling supported and valued. When individuals feel part of a team working towards a common goal, they are more likely to push themselves to new heights. This perfect combination fosters a culture of continuous improvement and innovation while tending to the human side at work. The great organizations that stand the test of time are ones that create sustainable systems that can be reproduced with new and existing colleagues or teammates. Make no mistake about it; the culture begins with the leader. However, as Dr. Joe Sanfelippo (2022) writes in "Lead from Where You Are," and best-selling author John Maxwell (2006) emphasizes in his work "The 360 Leader", everyone has a say and impact on the culture around you. You lead from where you are. Individually, we influence our environment.

## Chick-fil-A

Consider fast-food restaurants that you may regard as embodying the two pillars of an elite culture. What comes to mind? Entities like Chick-fil-A rise to the top, in my opinion. Why? Because they offer a good product, their chicken, combined with top-notch service and a positive culture. This includes friendly service with a smile and expressions of gratitude like, "It's my pleasure." No matter which Chick-fil-A restaurant you visit across the country, the experience is almost always the same, reflecting the systems in place throughout the organization. A relatively consistent experience awaits you, encompassing specific quality and consistency in the taste of the food and an environment created by its employees that consistently leaves you feeling good.

Elite cultures are not constructed overnight; they develop over time with daily dedication to refining systems, processes, and interpersonal interactions. Creating a consistent product and environment invariably arises as a result of effective leadership, emphasizing processes, products, and the environment.

This is achieved by hiring individuals with specific attributes, clearly communicating standards, providing training on processes, systems, and procedures related to the product, and fostering a consistent organizational culture. These cultures don't arise accidentally, nor do past experiences sustain them; instead, they result from intentional effort each day.

When it comes to establishing a high-level culture in business, Chick-fil-A places a strong emphasis on selecting operators who

embody specific qualities. As outlined by the Chick-fil-A corporation
on their main website (n.d.), these
individuals are expected to possess
specific characteristics to contribute
to their franchise's success and community impact. "Generally speaking,
we [Chick-fil-A] seek out restaurant Operators who are looking
for a full-time, 'hands-on' business
opportunity; have a proven track

> These cultures don't
> arise accidentally,
> nor do past
> experiences sustain
> them; instead,
> they result from
> intentional effort
> each day.

record in business leadership; have successfully managed their personal
finances; are results-oriented self-starters interested in growing a business; strive to be community leaders; and are prepared to have no other
active business ventures."

Chick-fil-A is known for several positive aspects that contribute to
its success and positive public perception. Here they are listed under
the Pillar 1 and 2 format:

### Pillar 1 - High Standards for Chick-fil-A:

+ **Quality Products:** The company strongly emphasizes the quality of its food. Fresh and high-quality ingredients contribute to
  a positive dining experience.
+ **Consistent Brand Image:** Chick-fil-A has built a consistent and
  positive brand image. This includes the company's commitment
  to community involvement, values-driven approach, and fami-
  ly-friendly atmosphere.
+ **Innovative Marketing:** Chick-fil-A has been successful in creating memorable marketing campaigns. The clever use of the
  cow mascot and campaigns like "Eat Mor Chikin" have become
  iconic.

* **Efficient Drive-Thru Operations:** Chick-fil-A is known for its fast and efficient drive-thru service, which contributes to customer convenience.

### Pillar 2 - Positive Environment for Chick-fil-A:

* **Customer Service Excellence:** Chick-fil-A is renowned for its exceptional customer service. The staff is courteous and attentive, and they go the extra mile to make customers feel valued.
* **Closed on Sundays:** The decision to remain closed is based on the founder's beliefs. While it may be unconventional in the fast-food industry, it has contributed to the company's reputation for standing by its values.
* **Employee Training and Satisfaction:** Chick-fil-A invests in training its employees and emphasizes their satisfaction. This is reflected in the positive attitudes and service provided by staff members.
* **Community Involvement:** The company actively participates in community initiatives and charitable work. This commitment to giving back contributes to a positive public perception.

These takeaways showcase the importance of customer-centric values, product quality, brand consistency, and community engagement in Chick-fil-A's success.

## Insights from Chick-fil-A Restaurant Owner-Operator: Louie's Story

I interviewed a successful Chick-fil-A owner-operator, Louie Murillo, who oversees multiple restaurants in the Dallas-Fort Worth metroplex in Texas. I gained valuable insights into the specific criteria for establishing an elite culture. Louie's experience sheds light on how these criteria foster a highly profitable business (high standards) and play a pivotal role in retaining employees (positive environment), ensuring the longevity of the elite culture. Louie is known for his exceptional ability to retain talent and foster a thriving work culture. In addition to the franchise's standards, he unveiled some essential strategies contributing to his elite workplace environment.

As a significant morale contributor, Louie emphasizes celebrating every aspect of his team's journey, recognizing achievements, and making everyone feel valued.

Louie says the "key to success lies in creating a culture where leaders are grown from within." He believes in "celebrating various milestones, such as birthdays, anniversaries, and promotions, to ensure each team member feels acknowledged and appreciated." Louie goes beyond the workplace, showing sensitivity to family needs and allowing employees to prioritize family obligations. If someone's child is sick, he understands and assists the "team member" in allowing them time off to take care of their child's needs. Naturally, there cannot be an abuse of this time off.

One distinctive approach Louie takes is implementing a yearly theme for his employees; for instance, this year's theme is "What you do matters." This thematic approach helps draw attention to detail, fostering mutual recognition among team members for each other's strengths. Louie emphasizes that this recognition is not solely leadership-driven but encourages peer-to-peer acknowledgment, ensuring everyone feels engaged and valued.

Highlighting the positives contributing to success, Louie accentuates the importance of replicating successful behaviors within the team. He says this positive reinforcement is crucial in maintaining a high-performing and engaged workforce.

Louie attributes his Chick-fil-A's success to its "people," stating, "It comes down to our people. It's 100% our people, and without the people, you can't execute." His approach to employee support involves coaching and creating growth opportunities. By actively coaching his team members, Louie's team enhances the overall guest experience, emphasizing the importance of investing in the professional development of his employees.

Regarding hiring, Louie seeks individuals with growth potential. He focuses on helping them evolve into leaders within the restaurant, providing constant coaching to ensure they perform at the desired level. His commitment to creating opportunities and fostering a positive work culture exemplifies Chick-fil-A's dedication to maintaining an elite status within the industry. Always eager to be of service, Louie reminds me as we end the interview that, "It's my pleasure to help," knowing that investing in others benefits everyone.

### Reflection:

1. What does my culture of high standards look and sound like?
2. What takeaways from the Chick-fil-A examples can contribute to my own positive environment?

## Culture is Fragile

Culture can be compared to a delicate object susceptible to breakage if not handled carefully. Think of it as a fragile vase, glass, or plate—something that, if dropped, can break. You inherit this delicate object if you're new to a culture. A misstep, a wrong move, can crack or even break it. Beginning with a new culture involves picking up the good and bad pieces and carefully crafting something new. Sometimes, the culture you become a part of can thrive, requiring continuous focused attention to sustain its greatness. However, in certain situations, the existing culture may be fractured or broken, and building a new one from scratch becomes necessary to achieve the desired goals.

For those who have been part of a culture for a short duration, you add decorative layers to the object. It takes a visual shape and starts to look a certain way. You add to it with decor, giving it appearances that may change over the years. If the culture in which you serve is broken and you lack the influence to restore it, you will need to decide whether to stay and exert influence to improve it or find a new culture to be a part of altogether. If you become the leader of the culture, it is your responsibility to set the vision and mission and create the core values to enhance the culture to where it needs to be improved. This may require removing the broken pieces of the culture to gain new elements that will positively contribute to a new and improved culture.

Regardless of when you come into possession of this fragile cultural object, it's vulnerable to the hits and bumps of daily life. Sometimes, it might develop cracks, and, in unfortunate cases, it can shatter. The analogy extends to culture, requiring constant maintenance and protection of its fragile state. Every action and every decision contribute to its form, making it a collective responsibility to ensure it remains intact, vibrant, and resilient. How are you tending to and shaping your cultural object today?

## Reflection:

As you contemplate your journey and culture development, some pivotal questions emerge:

1. What do you envision an ideal culture to resemble?
2. Take a moment to think: What does that look like specifically?
3. How do individuals treat one another in that type of culture?
4. What are the shared expectations?
5. What do the daily actions and behaviors of the individuals within the culture convey?

# CHAPTER 3

~

# Elite Mission and Vision

## Have a Vision and Mission; It's Your Compass

Education is one of the most critical elements of a thriving society. With technological advancements, including the advancement of artificial intelligence (AI) and remote work opportunities on the rise, the need to re-envision what education should look like is more important today than ever. We must work together to shape a better future for education, embracing various perspectives and solutions to create a supportive learning environment for every student. That is why elite cultures focus on specific goals they aim to accomplish.

A clear vision of your destination is crucial for success in any endeavor. You must have a vision of where you are going, laying the foundation for creating a roadmap to achieve your goals.

You may lack direction and purpose without a clear vision of your destination. Making informed decisions and taking actions that align with your desired outcomes becomes challenging. Without a vision, you are aimlessly driving to an unknown destination.

A clear vision is a guiding force that helps you understand where you want to go and why. It provides a sense of clarity, motivation, and focus. Coupled with a mission, you can set specific goals, develop strategies, and make choices that move you closer to your desired destination.

A vision statement can hold significance as it functions as a road-map for success. It serves as a guiding light when employees, students, athletes, etc., face challenges and acts as a source of motivation, inspiring them to collaborate towards common objectives.

The mission is simply why you exist and what you want to accomplish at your core. Keep the mission simple.

## BEST–Building Excellent Schools (Today) Together

The Colorado Department of Education has strategically crafted its mission, encapsulating its educational focus through the succinct *Building Excellent Schools Today* (BEST) acronym. Beyond being a mere acronym, BEST signifies a robust commitment to creating exemplary educational spaces, guaranteeing optimal environments for our students to flourish and learn. In a parallel narrative, a Texas school district consistently ranks among the state's academic and extracurricular elites, once exemplifying its mission statement also using the acronym *BEST*, which stands for *Building Excellent Schools Together*. Its simplicity and core mission made it highly impactful in day-to-day work. The district's mission, crafted by Dr. Robin Ryan, the superintendent at the time, created a straightforward approach for everyone to be the best by working together as a unified school community.

This mission was not burdened with length or complexity, making it effortlessly memorable and allowing schools to stay focused. It was compelling because it kept all stakeholders firmly rooted in the "why" of their purpose: to construct exceptional schools. It emphasized the importance of collective effort and consideration for every stakeholder involved, reinforcing their commitment to work together towards a common goal.

What is your overall mission for your class, school, district, team, or workplace? Find a simple rallying cry to remind everyone of the purpose and why behind the work.

## How to Create an Elite Mission Statement

Creating an elite mission for a class, school, or workplace involves thoughtful strategic planning with elements of the two pillars. The breakdown of BEST is as follows: Building Excellent (which represents Pillar 1: High Standards), and Together (which signifies the action, depicting how we execute the mission—Pillar 2: Positive Environment). Here are some strategies to help you develop a compelling elite mission statement:

1. Determine the ultimate purpose of the work in which you are investing.

2. Keep it Simple and Memorable: Craft a mission statement that is concise, straightforward, and memorable. Avoid jargon or complex language. A simple mission is easier for all organization members to communicate and internalize. Simply, why do you exist and what do you want to accomplish?

3. Make it Action-Oriented: Frame your mission statement to inspire action and guide behavior. Use action verbs and active language to convey a sense of urgency and commitment.

4. Communicate and Reinforce: Once the mission is established, communicate it consistently and effectively throughout the organization. Ensure all stakeholders, colleagues, and/or employees understand and embrace the mission. Regularly reinforce its importance and relevance in various communication channels and activities.

Remember, a great mission captures the essence of your organization's purpose, inspires action, and resonates with all stakeholders.

It should be a guiding light that drives decision-making and fosters a sense of unity and motivation.

## Harnessing Student Voice: Collaboratively Create Your Class Mission

As an educator or coach, consider how you can create a class/team mission statement that fosters shared ownership between students/athletes and the teacher/coach. Take time at the beginning of the school year or season to prioritize student voice and collaborate with them in defining the class mission and overall goals. Implementing this proven best practice will foster community, commitment, and alignment with your overarching mission and goals. It will cultivate an environment in which shared ownership of the journey becomes the norm. When your class, team, or staff completes the document, encourage members to sign a poster or banner with the mission statement. This signed commitment serves as a tangible reminder throughout the season or school year, emphasizing shared ownership and honoring the process toward achieving the shared mission.

## Reflecting on Your Vision and Mission and Next Steps

Are you a veteran in your role with an established mission? If so, reflect on the following questions:

1.  As a veteran in your role and a proven professional with an established vision and mission, how do you ensure the sustainability of your mission? How are you actively empowering and inspiring those around you to uphold and advance its principles? How are you weaving in your mission and vision throughout communication?

2. How do you effectively communicate and reinforce your mission to others, especially those new to your organization?

3. How do you mentor and guide other leaders in embracing and advancing the mission?

# CHAPTER 4

~

# Elite Core Values

## Building Elite Environments through Core Values

J ust as belief systems differ, your core values will also vary. When leading any organization, class, team, business, etc., you must know your core values to best guide the organization. Some organizations take a holistic approach, allowing their stakeholders to identify the organization's core values, while other times, the leader(s) establish the values and lead the organization with them in mind. Recognizing and reverting to an organization's core values is vital to helping people approach their day-to-day tasks. Core values will guide and focus individuals on how tasks should be approached. Core values must be *caught* more than they are

> Core values must be *caught* more than they are *taught*.

*taught.* They are "caught" by simply living out the core values of what you DO, not just what you SAY. You must lead by example and live out your core values, or they will die on the paper you wrote them on.

At Colleyville Middle School in Colleyville, Texas, the school team used their mission to shape the vision and goals for the school, aiming to achieve the highest levels of academic and extracurricular success. Despite the challenges faced in the post-pandemic educational landscape, the school not only survived, but thrived.

Staff members maintained high academic and extra-curricular standards at the school. It took the lead in education, increasing the school's impact recognized at the local, state, and national levels. With a clear mission and execution of their goals, the efforts of the stakeholders were recognized as the school earned prestigious titles such as "Texas Schools to Watch" by the Texas Association of Secondary School Principals and a Nationally Recognized Model Campus by the National Forum to Accelerate Middle-Grades Reform. The school consistently received an "A" rating in Texas, with a school year that experienced 100% of the students achieving at least one year's academic growth. The 100% growth is practically unheard of, as it represents that 100% of the students walking the halls gained at least a year of growth from their previous academic point, regardless of their background, circumstances, or educational levels of the past. The state accountability scores (Texas Education Agency, 2022) reached the highest figures in the school's state scoring history in several areas, including every grade level in reading, math (algebra), and science (biology). The school enhanced the connection between the greater school community and the staff, resulting in remarkable growth of the Parent-Teacher Association (PTA). Over the next five consecutive school years, the school achieved an unprecedented surge in PTA memberships. There were more members of the PTA than there were students each school year. With the intentionally unified vision and mission, the school community's efforts were acknowledged by the state and national PTA, honoring the school as a National PTA School of Excellence.

The accolades also reached into the fine arts programs, such as the band winning state and national awards, with a couple of years being the state runner-up in their classification. These achievements were attributed to a shared commitment to building excellence, using their school's core values as a guide. Their values were carefully woven into the institution's fabric during the hiring process, all professional development training, staff meetings, and daily interactions with one another.

The accolades directly reflected the commitment to the mission, high standards, and a positive school culture. The school created an environment in which excellence thrived due to a clear mission, vision, and core values centered on **positivity**, **teamwork**, **strengths**, and a **growth mindset**.

Positivity, the first core value, became the cornerstone of building a positive environment, fostering an environment where warmth and encouragement set the tone for daily interactions. Growth Mindset, the second core value, became the driving force behind high standards, emphasizing continuous improvement and learning, pushing staff and students to achieve their best.

The third and fourth core values, Strengths, and Teamwork, transcended both pillars of an elite culture. Strengths highlighted individuals' unique talents, contributing to a positive environment and high standards. The fourth core value, Teamwork, emphasized collaboration and unity, reinforcing the commitment to excellence in all endeavors.

The school's remarkable achievements were not accidental but resulted from a collective adherence to these core values. Intentionality with everything was key. For those seeking inspiration, Colleyville Middle School's core values provide a robust template for cultivating and sustaining an elite culture. Let's look at their core values:

**"Intentionality with everything is key."**

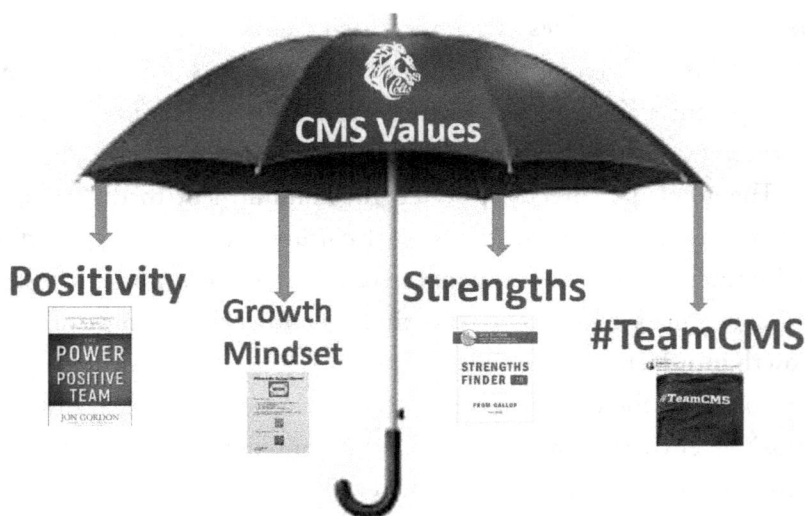

**CMS Values**

Positivity — Growth Mindset — Strengths — #TeamCMS

## Core Value #1: Positivity

Positivity was reinforced in the culture through Jon Gordon's influential works, particularly *The Energy Bus* (2007) and *The Power of a Positive Team* (2018). They formed a cornerstone of the desired culture that became a part of daily interactions from morning drop-off to the time students left to go home. Regular book studies anchored the staff in the power of positive mindsets, fostering a pervasive atmosphere of optimism. This intentionality manifested in daily interactions, from the warm greeting in the front office to every encounter in the building. You could genuinely sense the positivity from your initial interaction at the front office, through walking the halls, and engaging with kind and helpful staff members. The team was steadfast in creating a positive atmosphere.

Even after immense success in overall school scores and accolades, the staff worked to maintain a positive environment by adopting another proven program, *The Energy Bus for Schools* (Gordon & Van Allan, 2024). Along with CharacterStrong's character curriculum, these impactful programs successfully ingrained the desired behavior within the school community. Staff, students, and the broader school community consistently demonstrated respect, kindness, and understanding in their interactions. Positive character development was incorporated into the advisory period and throughout the school day to help promote a positive atmosphere.

This didn't mean that every encounter was positive; however, every meeting and conversation began from a place of presuming positive intent. When negativity reared its head, the pillar of having high standards expected every team member to confront and remove the negativity to reset into a positive place. This approach became applicable in every situation led by the leaders at the school, eventually becoming a way of daily life for all who would walk the halls at the school. The core value of positivity anchored everything they did.

## Core Value # 2: Growth Mindset

A second core value the school adopted was having a Growth Mindset. Growth Mindset was embraced as a fundamental belief—that every student could grow academically—and was modeled by staff members, who could also evolve and improve. Modeling this mentality during professional development and meetings became pivotal, ensuring students mirrored these desired behaviors of working hard to become better.

A shared understanding permeated the culture, emphasizing that whether it was someone's 1st

A shared understanding permeated the culture, emphasizing that whether it was someone's 1st or 31st year in education, continuous professional and personal growth was achievable for everyone.

or 31st year in education, continuous professional and personal growth was achievable for everyone. Having a growth mindset was the standard for all. It's important to note that experience was highly valued and acknowledged, providing guidance for new educators in mentoring roles. This celebration of experience did not diminish the importance of growth for all; instead, the culture encouraged the idea that ongoing improvement was attainable and beneficial for the entire community. Even learning a small nugget of information was considered a win for any staff member.

## Core Value #3: Strengths

A third core value incorporated into the culture was Strengths. In particular, Gallup StrengthsFinder (Rath, 2007) enhances the performance of staff and students by identifying and capitalizing on their given strengths and talents. Strengths and talents were celebrated as integral aspects of the school's identity, and eventually, every single staff member and student would take the Gallup Strengths assessment (Rath, 2007). By focusing on individual and collective strengths, the staff fostered a culture in which each member and their contributions were valued. Instead of focusing on weaknesses, they elevated strengths and highlighted the talents of everyone. Learning and interacting with each staff member's strengths, lifting their talents, and observing how they approached their work and relationships with colleagues helped create a sense of empathy, trust, and awareness. This understanding extended beyond the workplace, influencing daily interactions among colleagues. Understanding each other's strengths also provided insight into individuals' perspectives, contributing to the ability to presume positive intent based on understanding what team members valued. With a deeper knowledge of one another, people could collaborate more effectively and at the highest levels.

## Core Value #4: Teamwork

Finally, the school focused on a team concept, knowing that two minds were better than one, three better than two, etc. Ultimately, the school was stronger when everyone involved committed to the school culture as individuals with unique strengths and talents to be better for one another as a whole, working towards the same mission. The culmination of the efforts emphasized collaboration, unity, and shared goals, which contributed to the overall school culture and ultimately led to greater success for the staff, students, and school community.

Incorporating these core values into daily school life required consistent communication and relentless modeling. From daily conversations to newsletters to staff meetings and professional development days, interactions with one another, to messages sent out, the core values were embedded in every aspect of communication. However, it wasn't just about catching the core values; the hiring process, which we will focus on later in the book, became a strategic tool to bring individuals on board who also embodied the core values. This intentional infusion of values became the heartbeat of the school culture, shaping a vibrant and positive environment. Elements of the core values all contributed to either pillar 1, high standards or pillar 2, positive environment.

## Core Values in Practice: A Championship Journey

When Coach Smith assumed the role of Athletic Coordinator at a new school, the athletic program was in dire straits. The football team had only secured one victory in the preceding two years, while basketball and track and field also struggled to remain competitive. Compounding the challenges, there had been significant turnover within the coaching staff.

Rather than viewing this situation as a setback, the coach saw it as an opportunity for transformation. Instead of being disheartened by the need to rebuild the coaching staff, there was excitement about shaping a new team with a shared mission and core values. Recognizing the importance of fostering competition, positivity, and a fun, engaging atmosphere, the focus shifted towards instilling these core values throughout the program.

Collaborating closely with the school principal, efforts were made to recruit a new teaching-coaching staff aligned with these values. Understanding that an elite culture required individuals who could elevate the program, emphasis was placed on hiring those who understood the importance of building students of good character and learning how to win guided by the values. High-level leaders understand that hiring people with varying strengths and talents will elevate everyone's focus. This strategic approach to staffing underscored the commitment to excellence.

With the introduction of these core values, a noticeable transformation occurred within the program. Practices became more competitive, focusing on simulating game-day scenarios to adequately prepare student-athletes. In elite environments, intentionality is the secret sauce that can help transform everything into excellence. Moreover, the strength of positivity became evident as coaches and athletes alike embraced a culture of encouragement and celebration. The strength of positivity looked different in everyone based on their own strengths and talents.

This positivity extended to creating a fun, engaging environment in which moments of celebration were woven into the program's fabric. From pumping high-energy music into locker rooms to fostering a sense of camaraderie among teammates, every effort was made to make the athletic experience enjoyable while maintaining high-performance standards. Football, like other work-environments, can be hard. A space was created that took the mind off of the rough grind that football can be and changed the mindset to having fun while going to work in a highly competitive and demanding environment.

> In elite environments, intentionality is the secret sauce that can help transform everything into excellence.

Integral to this transformation was recognizing the value of mentorship and second chances. Coach Smith felt that one of the best things a student could have was a mentor to guide them. He thought that students like himself needed positive mentors to help them through their impressionable years and provide them with opportunities for correction and growth. The next generation will be influenced by their mentors. The question is not *whether* the next generation will find mentors; the question is: *what kind* of mentors will they find? Drawing from personal experiences, the coach emphasized the importance of providing guidance and support to students, particularly during their formative years. This commitment to nurturing growth created a culture in which mistakes were seen as learning and personal development opportunities.

> The question is not *whether* the next generation will find mentors; the question is: *what kind* of mentors will they find?

Despite initial skepticism by returning staff members, these efforts yielded remarkable results. In the first year, the new coaching staff and student-athletes would win more than half the football games on the schedule, a couple of basketball championships, and a Track and Field championship. It was done with the same caliber of student-athletes who had won only a single football game in the previous two school years and were not taken seriously in any other sport in the athletics program. In three years, the athletics program secured 33% of all sports championships dating back to the school's opening in 1959. This success not only transformed the athletics program but also had a ripple effect throughout the school community. Pride and unity permeated the campus as students and staff rallied behind the program.

## Core Values Launch

Once your core values are established, lead from your position within the organization and set an example for everyone on the team, whether it's a class, team, school, district, or business. As architects of your mission and vision, your team must embody the core values in every action and decision. Leading by example is not just a slogan; it forms the foundation of cultural transformation. Be relentless in instilling the core values into the daily DNA of your team.

### *Guiding Questions for Implementing Core Values:*

1. Establishing your core values:
   + Do you have an established set of core values? If so, what does daily life say about your culture, and does it match your values?
2. Communication and Awareness:
   + Can your team members, including your colleagues, clearly articulate the core values?

- How are core values communicated to new team members?
- Is there a formal onboarding process that emphasizes the importance of these values?

3. Leadership Exemplification:
   - Are there mechanisms to recognize and celebrate individuals or teams that embody the core values?

4. Continuous Improvement and Reflection:
   - How does the organization (or you) solicit stakeholders' feedback regarding the effectiveness and impact of the core values?

5. Learning from Examples:
   - How might your organization learn from the examples mentioned in weaving core values into the institution's fabric?

## CHAPTER 5

~

# Elite Strengths

## Tapping into Strengths: Sylvester's Story

Sylvester was a student who frequently moved from school to school, occasionally getting into fights in his neighborhood when street games with local kids took an unexpected turn. Despite his challenges, he was the kind of kid all the other students wanted on their team during recess—sought after for his athletic abilities and competitive spirit. School success for Sylvester depended on the engagement level of the assignments and teachers. If interested, he excelled; otherwise, he could be the type of student who could be challenging for his teachers when bored.

I remember learning about Sylvester, a student whose 4th grade teacher, Mrs. Kicks, brought out his best by leveraging his strengths. Sylvester's teacher unknowingly tapped into his competitive nature through a school-wide competition using a mascot coincidentally resembling Sylvester, the cat from the Looney Tunes network. The Compu-Cat program focused on improving math fluency in students. Every week, students took a short quiz on learned math facts, progressing through levels upon mastery. The twist that engaged Sylvester was using different colored half-sheet quizzes, indicating varying math skills and levels. Like a video game, Sylvester was captivated by the desire to level up. This unintentional competition sparked a drive in Sylvester to be the best in the class. Eagerly anticipating new colors each week, he bought into the competition and wanted to stay at the top, mastering each concept and getting a new color each week. The mere prospect of a new color and level motivated Sylvester to study and grasp math concepts that the rest of the class wouldn't encounter for another two years.

His teacher masterfully differentiated for him and provided one-on-one instruction as he surpassed the rest of the class, eagerly anticipating the unveiling of the new color of the test at the end of the week. Mrs. Kicks would employ a high-leverage teaching strategy called "aggressive monitoring," which involved systematically checking on all her students as they worked on new academic concepts while strategically ensuring overall desired on-task behavior. She began her first pass around the class, starting with Sylvester, checking to ensure he understood the week's new academic concept. If he did, she knew that the information was adequately taught. If there was any confusion, she would immediately see it in Sylvester and know she would need to re-teach the entire class. As she came around to Sylvester a second time, she would have the opportunity to teach him a new concept since he had mastered the previous one while the other students continued where they were.

At the end of the school year, Sylvester was crowned the Compu-Cat king, recognized as the top math student in the entire school, including older 5th-grade students. His teacher's simple strategy of turning math into a friendly competition tapped into Sylvester's strength of competition and fueled his determination to excel. Sylvester's true story illustrates how leveraging an individual's strengths can drive success to elite levels.

## The Culture Starts Within: Shaping Your Environment through Self-Aware Strengths

Like Sylvester, we all possess unique strengths. Tapping into the strengths of others will help bring out the best in them, and understanding their strengths is crucial for effective influence. Regardless of where and what you are doing in life, knowing the strengths of those around you will benefit them and yourself. This brings us to the next important point in creating the best environment and culture you desire: understanding your own strengths.

The first step is knowing your strengths and talents and understanding how to use them in various environments, whether at home or work. You can't *grow yourself* without *knowing yourself*. By knowing your own strengths, you will also gain insight into how they might be perceived as weaknesses.

> You can't *grow yourself* without *knowing yourself.*

Self-awareness is the first step in your journey of growth. For example, Sylvester's highly competitive drive may be a turn-off to others who share a different level of competitiveness. It's essential to recognize that your strengths can also have potential downsides.

Using Sylvester as an example, his competitive drive motivates and facilitates learning, as seen in the math competition. That is a good thing. However, it's wise to consider whether this strength could be perceived as a weakness, such as boasting or taunting others during any kind of competition. In Sylvester's case, he didn't approach it negatively, but the potential was there.

Regardless, do not let others' opinions of your strengths deter you from your mission. Sylvester should focus on using his strengths constructively and positively, regardless of others' opinions. It's essential not to be deterred by naysayers. Instead, be a cheerleader for others in their pursuit of success, especially if they are on your team. That is critical. Just ensure that you're using your strengths for the greater good.

This example underscores the importance of being aware of your strengths and talents and understanding how others might perceive them as weaknesses, potentially affecting your influence. A key component of building elite cultures starts with us as individuals. We need to look internally to understand how we contribute to the environments and cultures being built or sustained. Your culture begins with you.

## You Have Unique Strengths

Our world needs leaders; it needs you! We all possess unique strengths and talents that set us apart. In various ways, everyone assumes a leadership role in life. Today, more than ever, our families, friends, communities, country, and the world require the best version of ourselves. Make no mistake: your culture begins with you. Own it. It is your life; ultimately, you are responsible for your actions and your effect on your world.

A great starting point is to recognize that your personal strengths are typically innate qualities you have within you, distinguishing you from others. It's not necessarily just knowledge-based or learned behavior but can be refined and honed through practice. What distinctive strengths and talents can you share with the world? Our life experiences mold our reality and daily interactions with others. Your life is unique, and your significance and influence reach beyond yourself. No one is a greater expert on your strengths and talents than you. You are the only person on this earth

> Your life is unique, and your significance and influence reach beyond yourself. No one is a greater expert on your strengths and talents than you.

with your God-given abilities. You don't require a particular title or status to make an impact; you influence daily, often without even realizing it. Choose to lead yourself wisely.

Consider the wise old saying: "Everybody is a genius. But if you judge a fish by its ability to climb a tree, it will live its whole life believing it is stupid." While the origin of this saying is debated, with some attributing it to Albert Einstein, its message is profound. Focusing on your strengths rather than weaknesses significantly increases your chances of success and a successful culture.

## Gallup Strengths

The Gallup organization is a leader in global analytics, which has revealed that "people who use their strengths every day are three times more likely to report having an excellent quality of life, six times more likely to be engaged at work, 8% more productive and 15% less likely to quit their jobs." (Gallup, 2015). Capitalizing on your talents and strengths will allow you to function well in your faith, family, work, and life. Tasks will not seem like "work" when you are using your strengths.

There are many resources to help you discover your talents and strengths, and I have found that Gallup's Strengths is one of those great resources. The Gallup CliftonStrengths assessment (2015) helps uniquely pinpoint your strengths. The analytics in the assessment have been refined over time, as over 26 million people have taken it since 1999. Using sources like CliftonStrengths, which breaks down the detailed analytics given in your responses, helps lift your strengths, allowing you to better realize your talents and use them intentionally in your daily life.

As described in the earlier chapter, certain aspects of your strengths can be incorporated into your core values. By intertwining your strengths into your core values, you will discover that the various tasks in your life become easier to accomplish.

## Unlocking Elite Potential: Harnessing Strengths for Excellence in Education

Lauren's school harbored a wealth of untapped talent among its staff and students. Teachers in her school were stuck in a rut with reused lessons dating back over a decade, indicated by the date in the bottom corner of worksheets passed out to students. They needed help engaging their compliant students. As a teacher-leader, Lauren discovered the Gallup book *Teach with Your Strengths* (Gallup Inc., 2005) successfully incorporated strengths into her teaching. She created an engaging and enjoyable learning environment in her classroom by integrating game elements like points, badges, and leaderboards, fostering collaboration and interaction while implementing healthy competition among her students.

Upon Lauren's transition to a leadership role, her principal embraced the Strengths model. Initiating a book study with support from the leadership team, the school expanded the Strengths assessment and study to the broader leadership team, eventually reaching every teacher, staff member, and student on campus. Adopting a school-wide focus on strengths rather than weaknesses, the environment flourished with increased classroom engagement, a positive relational culture, and enriched professional development days, staff meetings, and classrooms.

During one school year, it was discovered that a majority of students at a specific grade level possessed the strength of competition as one of their top talents. The teachers in that grade level strategically incorporated competitive activities throughout their classes, hallways, and in the school, resulting in highly engaging learning experiences and, inadvertently, an overall fun learning environment. The shift elevated student engagement and enhanced the rigor of academic activities, creating additional student-centered learning environments.

By centering the school environment around individuals' unique strengths, staff and students learned how to excel as students, communicators, teammates, and problem solvers. The emphasis on the human element and individual strengths contributed to a positive and flourishing educational community.

## Building Community Through Strengths

At one school renowned for its strong connection among leaders, teachers, and staff members, meetings kick off with connection activities tailored to each individual's strengths. These exercises serve as ice-breakers and relationship enhancers, fostering a sense of community and empathy among colleagues. Administrators lead these activities in their weekly leadership meetings. Later, the entire staff engages in quick warm-up exercises during their staff meetings to promote inclusivity of personalities and a receptive mindset. This positive atmosphere persists even on long days following strenuous school hours, as relationships are bolstered by mutual recognition of each staff member's strengths, contributing to an overall positive environment. These activities are replicated during professional learning community (PLC) meetings and professional development days. Visitors to the staff meetings and PLCs frequently comment on the palpable sense of goodwill in the room, which is uncommon in other places they visit.

By understanding your own and others' personal strengths, you can tap into their power and use them in your day-to-day life and work interactions to benefit yourself and those around you.

### Reflection:

1.  How do you leverage your talents in your professional environment?
2.  What energizes you?

CHAPTER 6

~

# Elite Team

## Hiring for Your Culture: It's 100% the People

As a leader, the journey through various stages of the hiring process will unfold. Initially, you step into the role of a positional leader, where individuals follow you out of necessity due to your position—that's a positional leader. Building relationships comes next, as you get to know your team and they walk alongside you—that's a relational leader. As you consistently deliver high-quality work, people become more willing to follow you based on your productivity and performance—an effective leader. Ultimately, after establishing success and credibility, your investment in others takes hold, raising them in status and position, leading to followers who trust your leadership—that's an elite leader. Over time, high-quality cultures can be cultivated with intentionality. This, in turn, simplifies the hiring process, as individuals are drawn to join what has been established. The appeal lies in the environment that has been nurtured and people's desire to be part of it.

The timeline involved in building trust and credibility as a leader means that organizations will experience different cultural phases. When you're a new leader, culture-building can be gradual unless you're working with many new team members, which can accelerate cultural development. That may sound counter-intuitive, but having many new team members presents the advantage of simultaneously conducting the same team-building exercises, fostering a common bond among the new team. The initial impression made during these events is powerful and usually can't be replicated in the future due to the significance of those initial team-building moments. They can be added upon later with new staff members, but the initial experience and moments are unique and challenging to replicate. However, for most situations involving new leaders, the process takes time.

As you consistently reinforce and communicate your core values and take action that aligns with them, the culture gradually evolves and takes shape over time. For veteran leaders, the established culture and the timeline of individuals' growth provide opportunities to empower emerging leaders. This allows them to lead while you guide the path, engage in big-picture planning, set goals, and envision the future.

## Fostering a Culture of Shared Expectations and Standards

Ensuring that the right individuals fill your organization's appropriate roles is paramount. Surrounding yourself with like-minded individuals who share your work or team goals is a strategy that can consistently yield positive outcomes. Having colleagues who share a similar mission does not compromise individual talents or the unique skills they bring to the team; instead, it enhances the overall experience for everyone involved.

Harvard Business Review (Chamorro-Premuzic, 2022) sheds light on fascinating workplace dynamics, revealing that proximity to high performers can significantly boost your productivity by 15%. On the flip side, being in close quarters with a low performer might lead to a staggering 30% decrease in your productivity. The pinnacle of achievement is reached when colleagues, coaches, teammates, and others align their expectations with a similar unwavering commitment to performing at the highest levels possible. As leaders, it is our responsibility to ensure that team members are introduced to the expectations and standards that have been established.

It's never safe to assume that someone inherently understands their role or knows how to navigate the culture. We must provide clear communication to new team members early and consistently. This ensures that they adapt well and contribute to the culture in alignment with the high standards and collaborative engagement with others.

## Navigating Personnel Change

Change is not always bad—but it can be. Regarding personnel, turnover is inevitable; individuals depart for various reasons, including relocating for family, promotions, or, unfortunately, facing life crises. Such changes are understandable and should not be seen as a reflection of the culture.

However, there is a distinction to be made. Suppose individuals choose to leave because their values do not align with the culture's values. In that case, it is likely in the individual's and the organization's best interest that they find another role elsewhere. This scenario often occurs when a new leader is in place, and there is a sense of nostalgia for previous leadership and the way things "used to be." The certainty of these thoughts and emotions is real, and it becomes a crossroads where the employee must decide whether to fully commit with a positive mindset or seek a new opportunity elsewhere.

Another realistic possibility is that the staff member stays around disgruntled, which is not in the best interest of the individual, organization, or the people with whom the employee interacts. Employees dissatisfied in the workplace significantly impact the culture, work environment, themselves, and those around them in a negative way.

Productivity can come to a screeching halt with individuals like this. It is to everyone's benefit that the individual leaves.

However, when influential individuals who are good for the overall culture leave for what appears to be a lateral or even a step-down role, primarily due to a workplace culture that doesn't align with their values, it can pose a concern for the organization. In such cases, thorough self-reflection by leadership and management should be undertaken in an effort to discern the reasons behind the departure and an analysis of what within the organization's culture is causing individual(s) to leave. Leadership team members need a growth mindset here, and egos should be set aside for critical reflection on the cause of losing such an effective person from the team. After reflection, actions to address and fix aspects of the culture that are within the control of leadership and caused the employee to leave should be considered to improve that portion of the culture. Frankly, this is what elite culture leaders do. They put their ego aside and genuinely consider why individuals leave the team. Again, some reasons are understandable, others are encouraged, while still others cause the leader to look hard at which elements of the culture could be adapted to improve.

## New Hire, New Opportunity

Regardless of the reasons for employee turnover, a vacancy presents an opportunity to bring in a new individual whose values align with the workplace's culture and core values, thereby contributing to and elevating the overall mission. Change is inevitable, and effective leaders view it as an opportunity when it occurs. If you're a leader in personnel influence and decision-making, what steps do you take to recruit the best candidates actively? Suppose your approach involves waiting for a vacancy and reacting with a job posting and subsequent steps. In that case, you need to catch up in the recruiting and hiring process, immediately placing yourself at a disadvantage in the race for new, effective talent. With the work shortage situation in a post-pandemic era, recruiting future hires actively is much more critical. High-level leaders are proactive, not reactive, and actively network and recruit throughout the year.

If you can establish a pipeline of future employees and team members, this should become an additional focal point for future hiring success. For example, it is crucial to assess high school future teacher programs that aim to recruit students, prepare them for possible roles in education, and instill excitement about the profession to enhance retention rates. A teacher preparation program at the secondary level is a great way to build a foundation for potential future employees.

Ultimately, the better the culture, the better the possibility of having a stream of future employees ready to join your team because of your team's reputation. This is another excellent reason to build and or maintain an elite culture.

## Streamlining the Hiring Process: Actionable Steps for Selecting Top Talent

Hiring exceptional talent is a hallmark of effective leaders, enabling them to elevate their teams. However, to be clear, the hiring process will not always guarantee finding the perfect candidate. If such a strategy existed, every organization would be aware of it, and its implementation would be widespread. No hiring process can guarantee a slam dunk with every prospect.

As I transitioned into the role of principal, one of the most valuable lessons I carried with me was the importance of hiring the best talent. In the post-COVID-19 world, where hiring shortages are prevalent across professions and industries, striking quickly to secure the best candidates has become an essential aspect of the hiring process.

Hiring is an art, and each person approaches it differently. In my experience serving on countless interviewing committees with other hiring decision-makers at the table, I have encountered employers who adopt a cold, non-relational demeanor toward applicants, rattling off job-specific questions without creating a welcoming environment. This approach needs to be updated to entice high-level talent. The candidate now has more options in a post-COVID-19 world than ever before. Candidates today are not just being interviewed; they are interviewing you as a prospective employer. I have often been told how candidates are drawn to certain schools over others due to the positive and welcoming interviewing atmosphere they experience. The interview experience was the difference maker in obtaining high-level talent. Let me reiterate: candidates chose our team over others repeatedly because of how they felt during the job interview. I've been told numerous times how they recalled their feelings after they left, which ultimately influenced their decision. Their decision. Talented employees typically have options.

Our hiring committee teams will deliberately maintain an approachable demeanor and ensure a warm and friendly atmosphere that reflects our daily environment, trying to create a genuine connection with each candidate. We believe that the most outstanding talent evaluates the job requirements and the hiring committee. Before the interview process, it is vital to remind the team that the applicant is also evaluating us. The traditional approach of going through a list of questions without fostering positive connections is less practical than the welcoming approach described.

Placing excessive reliance on a brief 25–45-minute interview can be misleading. Interviews themselves can be nerve-racking, and they can fail to represent individuals in their everyday operational state accurately. Considering the candidate's overall body of work and gathering insights from references is essential for a more comprehensive understanding. However, it's important to consider the information in the larger context, including the references themselves. Top talent can easily be mismanaged by individuals who hold a manager's title.

When individuals have a long-standing record of success, their work successes should be evaluated within their context and given proper consideration.

When it's time to hire, remember the following: Given today's workforce shortages in all professions, especially education, the interviewee is also interviewing YOU. If you decide to stick to the old ways of question-answer, question-answer, "Do you have any questions for us?" and then follow that with "See you later," there's a good chance the candidate will say, "See YOU later" as they likely have another job offer waiting for them. Ensure that your interview questions align with your core values and reflect how you engage with prospective employees throughout the interview process, including before, during, and after the interview.

To enhance the effectiveness of the hiring process and increase the likelihood of securing top talent, consider implementing the following:

1. The importance of smiling, being friendly, and creating a relaxed environment cannot be overstated. It significantly influences the candidate's experience and perception of the hiring process. It also helps put their minds at ease and allows their nerves to settle, giving a better representation of who they are.

2. Select committee members who align with the desired culture and values you aim to replicate. Ensure you provide clear instructions about how you would like the interview to be conducted.

3. Avoid including individuals who do not share your values or are solely present to fulfill a requirement, particularly for organizational political reasons. Their feedback will reflect something other than the staff you aspire to build, potentially leading the hiring committee to make the wrong hiring decision. As

a decision maker, understand your committee's possible biases as decisions are made. Keep your mission and culture at the forefront when making a hiring decision.

4. Assess Cultural Fit: During the interview, evaluate the candidate's qualifications and potential fit within the organization's culture and values. This will help ensure alignment and long-term compatibility.

5. Communicate Effectively: Maintain open and transparent communication with candidates throughout the process, providing timely updates and feedback. This demonstrates respect and professionalism, regardless of the outcome. Remember that a candidate who may not be the right fit for a current position could be the perfect fit for a future opportunity.

By implementing these actionable steps, you can enhance the efficiency and effectiveness of your hiring process, increasing the chances of selecting top talent who will contribute to your organization's success. Revamp the traditional interviewing process and create an environment that mirrors your desired culture. Seek out individuals who uphold high standards and will contribute to fostering a positive environment.

## Reflection:

1. What characteristics are you seeking in a new team member who will align well with your organizational culture?
2. What would those characteristics entail if you were to create a portrait of the ideal candidate for your team?

# CHAPTER 7

~

# *Elite Awareness*

## Preserving Excellence: The Significance of Retaining the Right Talent

Once your team consists of individuals committed to the mission and heading toward the same destination, it's crucial to focus on retaining them. However, suppose there are any "energy vampires," as Jon Gordon (2007, p. 73) describes in his book *The Energy Bus*, on your team, defined as those who drain positive energy and replace it with negativity. In that case, it's essential to help them become better team members and colleagues or guide them off the bus toward something they are more passionate about and connected with. As a leader, you are responsible for ensuring that the right people are on the bus, in the right bus seats, and the wrong ones are off the bus.

Once you have the right team in place, your efforts should be directed toward retaining the team as individuals and a whole. This not only saves you time on the back end—in terms of going through the hiring process, developing an understanding of your processes and systems, and integrating them into the established culture—but also costs lots of money for the re-development of the new hires that aren't always seen on paper or the bottom line of budgets. Retaining the proper personnel when possible will also ensure your organization's stability and continued growth.

Remember to emphasize retaining your best people and top talent. When you promote the wrong people, your best will leave. The value of your best people goes beyond numbers; they help set the tone for your culture and help move others around them toward your mission and goals. In a profession like education, where the pay structure typically doesn't align with most for-profit companies, which can offer substantial financial bonuses and personal pay raises, it's crucial to understand the individuals on your team. It is beneficial to discover external factors beyond their roles that provide motivation and a desire to continue working well.

> When you promote the wrong people, your best will leave.

If you're a colleague who recognizes an individual's importance and positive impact on the team, find ways to tap into their professional love language. Lead from wherever you are, and take the initiative to celebrate those around you. You don't have to be in a specific role to create a positive environment around yourself. The positive benefits of lifting others begins with you and have a twofold benefit. One, you elevate them, and two, you elevate yourself in the process. Be sure to spotlight the correct individuals contributing to the culture you are working to create and maintain. Highlight those who deserve recognition, not the "energy vampires" or negative people who bring down others and performance.

## Committed to Excellence: Stephanie's Story

Stephanie drives approximately one hour each way to the school where she teaches. Despite the proximity to other schools and tempting offers from different, better-paying school districts, Stephanie remains steadfastly committed to her school.

The school where she teaches English holds a special place in her heart. Her school boasts a positive environment that emphasizes professional growth and celebrates the achievements of its staff. It stands out as a workplace where educators are not just employees, but valued contributors to a supportive and thriving community.

Stephanie's dedication is not an isolated case. Many staff members reject enticing offers to stay at the school, while others have taken significant pay cuts to join the team, and she tells us why:

> During the interview process at my school, I found a precise alignment of my skills, strengths, and values with the school. The approach resonated with me—recognizing professionalism and directing me to excel.
>
> A crucial aspect of our school's success lies in our commitment to creating a positive environment. Our administration prioritizes building a sense of community during staff meetings fostering connections among team members.
>
> Moreover, we take pride in celebrating our staff. Peers and students regularly recognize our achievements, from classroom victories to personal milestones like birthdays. This culture of appreciation contributes significantly to my overall connection to the school.
>
> Also, our administrative team trusts me to perform my job at the highest levels. As a principal, you must be 100 percent transparent, build up your staff, truly empower your staff, and have unwavering faith in what your team can achieve for the students and each other.

*Despite the lengthy commute (an hour each way), I value the quality time I spend with my daughter during these car rides. The heart-to-heart conversations, radio tunes, and moments of decompression have become an integral part of my daily routine. Meaningful connections are worth more than a shorter commute or a higher salary at different schools.*

*The main thing with teaching, I believe, is that you find your fit, you find your family, and it doesn't matter if you take a slight pay cut or you have to drive a little bit farther. Quality of life is worth more.*

−Stephanie McAvoy, English Teacher

## Reflective Engagement Questions

How would you and those on your team respond to the following questions from Gallup's employee engagement survey at Gallup.com? (Gallup, n.d.).

1. "Do I have the materials and equipment necessary to perform my work effectively?"
2. "Over the past seven days, have I received recognition or praise for my commendable work?"
3. "At my workplace, do my opinions appear to hold significance?"

These three inquiries represent only a fraction of the twelve statements crucial for assessing employee engagement. (Gallup, n.d.) Elevated engagement and enhanced well-being contribute to a more content and healthier educator, teammate, colleague, and worker. Thus, their impact directly affects morale, staff, students, teammates, performance measures, and the overall culture.

Leaders, take a moment to reflect on these additional questions:

1. As a leader, can I confidently assert that my team has access to the necessary materials and equipment for their roles, fostering an environment conducive to practical work? What's your initial response when staff members request materials for their roles? Do you try to explore ways to respond positively, or does your mind automatically lean towards "No" or "Not right now"? Your initial reaction may reflect your mindset regarding requests from individuals. Understanding where your mind tends to go can provide insight, enabling you to continue finding ways to support those around you or prompting you to pause when individuals offer feedback or make requests, allowing you to understand better what they need from you as a leader.

   I consistently remind my staff that the students' success is also their success, and their success is ours as a school. Encourage those around you to thrive; it's what high-level cultures do for one another and the organization. Ultimately, everyone wins.

2. Over the last work week, have team members actively acknowledged and praised the commendable efforts of the staff, recognizing their contributions to the institution's success? If you manage a sizable staff and have limited time for whole group recognition, how do you harness the support of leaders around you?

   I ask all level leaders how they recognize those on their teams. Regarding workplace recognition, the second question of giving recognition and praise specifically refers to acknowledgment in general and not just directly from the supervisor. How does the team recognize each other?

3. In the professional space I cultivate, do I create an atmosphere in which team members' opinions and ideas are heard and perceived as valuable contributors to the decision-making process? Do staff members feel listened to, and do they believe their opinions matter?

    While not every suggestion needs to be implemented, the significance of being heard and having a voice matters.

## Addressing and Preventing Teacher Burnout

The alarming rates of burnout among K-12 education employees and those in higher education, as revealed by the National Association of Secondary Principals (NASSP) reports (NASSP, 2021), underscore a pressing concern. Teachers and principals in the education sector report higher burnout rates than their counterparts in any other industry. The challenges of navigating a constantly-evolving educational environment contribute significantly to this burnout.

Burnout can severely affect educators' well-being, leading to feelings of energy depletion, mental distance from the job, negativism, and reduced professional efficacy (Lee, n.d.). In essence, burnout typically translates to lower performance and diminished educator well-being, and it doesn't naturally fade away with time; it necessitates intervention. Here are proactive steps leaders can take to tackle teacher burnout:

1. Allocate time to give back to teachers. Scrutinize the demands placed on teachers and identify tasks that can be removed. Despite our best intentions to establish efficient systems, we might inadvertently complicate teachers' roles, depriving them of precious time. Prioritize the essentials, such as cultivating an engaging classroom, fostering positive relationships, and delivering excellent instruction.

My colleague, Travis, would often compare educators' workload to a full closet: he would say you must first remove some clothes to add more items. Essentially, our plates as educators are overflowing, and leaders need to intentionally remove items from their overfilled plates, especially if a new requirement of the educator is necessary. Sometimes, in our best intentions to create systems, we can inadvertently complicate them and make things worse for educators. It's important to scrutinize existing and new requirements and ask if they are necessary to improve the environment. If the new items will enhance education, great, but what's coming off the plate since you are adding the new item?

2.  Support staff should do just that: support teachers. Regardless of your support role, seek opportunities to assist teachers when they need help.

3.  Leaders, be visible. Increase your visibility. Whenever feasible, make an effort to be present and seen. Merely being visible to teachers creates a sense of support and prevents feelings of isolation. Regular visibility is crucial; being present requires intentional scheduling with your calendar. In a support role, find opportunities to be in classrooms, halls, and around campus. Teachers should also be visible to each other in the hallways, which has substantial positive effects on students, staff, and morale. Naturally, this also decreases undesired student behavior in the halls and improves the overall environment.

4.  Leaders, listen to work-related problems: Actively listen to team members, allowing them to express work-related challenges and concerns.

5. Give meaningful recognition: Acknowledge and appreciate teachers' efforts in meaningful ways, recognizing their contributions to the institution.

6. Make everyone's opinion count: Create a culture in which every team member's opinion is valued and considered in decision-making processes.

7. Create a culture of well-being: Prioritize educators' mental and physical well-being and foster a culture that supports a healthy work-life balance.

Teacher burnout is not an inevitable outcome. By integrating anti-burnout practices into institutional strategies, we actively promote development, growth, and thriving well-being among educators.

## Understanding and Nurturing Your Professional Love Language

When colleagues are fortunate to have individuals who believe in them and feed them with positive affirmation, their longevity and engagement in their roles increase. This is true for every single person on your team and organization.

Positive words of affirmation are part of the love language, as described by Dr. Gary Chapman, a well-known counselor and founder of The 5 Love Languages concept (Chapman, 1992). When individuals receive encouragement, it fuels and motivates them to press on. Have you been someone's encouragement and fuel lately? According to Chapman (1992), everyone has a personal love language, and people should surround themselves with individuals who encourage and push them forward during the inevitable difficult times in their profession and personal life. Knowing your love language and being around people who positively feed your soul will motivate you during good times and bad. Investing in others with love and care is one of the most extraordinary acts we can do for others.

Remember that your love language might not be the same as others, so don't confuse the encouragement that you may seek with the same needs of those around you. Just because you may like receiving words of affirmation doesn't mean those around you need it as much as you do. Instead, they may appreciate acts of service, quality time, gifts, or physical touch like high fives or fist bumps.

At one school I have visited, the leadership team adopts a unique approach to fostering appreciation among its staff. During a culture-building segment of the leadership meeting, they start by identifying the "love language" of each staff member and reviewing a specific group of people each week (or sometimes bi-weekly), such as science teachers, allowing them to become acquainted with each staff member's unique love language. That's right, they have dedicated time built into their leadership meeting to help sustain their thriving culture. You might believe that this isn't the work educators should be engaged in, but I'm telling you, based on the results of schools like this, this *is* important work. Building culture while maintaining high standards in daily processes *is* the work.

The staff members' love languages are incorporated into the school's "family directory" I will explain in further detail later. Throughout the week, the leadership team goes the extra mile to express appreciation for the targeted group. Other staff members use the directory at any time to tailor their actions to resonate with their colleagues' professional love languages. This intentional effort creates a culture where team members feel valued and appreciated, directly contributing to boosted morale.

**Reflection:**

1. What is your love language?
2. Do you know the love language of those around you?
3. How do you fill others' emotional buckets when they may be low or empty?

If you haven't done so already, consider taking a free "5 Love Languages" quiz (Chapman, 1992) to understand your needs better and encourage others around you to do the same so you may learn one another better. (Visit: https://5lovelanguages.com/quizzes/love-language to take the quiz). Next, take action and apply your knowledge. This time-proven strategy functions effectively as part of the people culture you build and maintain around you. Now, let's explore additional ways to implement these strategies effectively.

## Understanding and Applying the Five Love Languages in Education: Jason's Story

Jason is a dynamic educator who always knows how to connect with students. He has pillar two down pat, building a thriving environment in all his classes. Jason understood that connections with his students were the key to his success, and one of the ways he achieved that was by understanding the Love Language concept from an educational lens as a teacher. Here is his story about the impact this can have on creating a robust student environment:

*I always considered myself a decent teacher who truly understood his students until that day when I walked into a classroom and asked a young lady at the front if she enjoyed sitting at that table full of boys. I always liked to start the class with humor, so the response was great when she shrugged and said, "Yes." The class thought it was a clever response and laughed like middle schoolers. I asked her a few follow-up questions, "Do you want to move seats, or do you want to stay there? Is this spot OK, or would you rather sit with some of your other friends?". She replied "Yes" to all my questions. I am sure there was a giant question mark over my head when one of the boys in the class said, "I don't think she speaks English." If I could have disappeared at that moment, I would have. I was embarrassed because I was trying to help her, but despite my best efforts, I could not get through to her. That young lady made me realize that it didn't matter how hard I tried to communicate with her; if I was speaking a language she did not understand, it was pointless.*

*That day changed me. I became consumed with meeting students' needs to provide them with the tools they needed to succeed. I stumbled upon a book I had read years ago, The 5 Love Languages by Dr. Gary Chapman (1992). Instead of seeing the love languages through a romantic lens, I looked at them through a relational lens and questioned how it might make me a better teacher. For several reasons, I understood better that the five love languages—words of affirmation, acts of service, receiving gifts, quality time, and physical touch—are crucial in education. Firstly, recognizing and catering to students' individual love languages can significantly enhance their sense of belonging and connectedness within the learning environment. By expressing appreciation and affirmation in ways that resonate with each student, educators can foster a supportive atmosphere conducive to academic growth and emotional well-being.*

*Secondly, incorporating the concept of love languages into education promotes inclusivity and equity. Students come from diverse backgrounds with varying cultural norms and personal preferences regarding how they give and receive love. By acknowledging and respecting these differences, educators can create a more inclusive classroom where every student feels valued and understood, regardless of their unique love language. Moreover, understanding students' love languages can inform instructional strategies and classroom management techniques. For instance, a student whose primary love language is quality time may benefit from one-on-one interactions with the teacher or small group discussions. In contrast, students who respond to acts of service may thrive when given opportunities to contribute to classroom projects or assist their peers. Tailoring teaching methods to align with students' love languages can enhance engagement and motivation, leading to improved academic outcomes.*

*Integrating the five love languages into education nurtures positive relationships between students and teachers. When educators demonstrate care and appreciation in ways that resonate with each student, they cultivate trust and rapport, which are essential for effective teaching and learning. By fostering solid interpersonal connections, educators can create a supportive learning community where students feel safe to take risks, ask questions, and collaborate with their peers.*

–Jason Cornelius, Former AVID Teacher and Counselor

## Best Friend at Work

Another statistically proven measurement by Gallup for employee engagement is that of an individual having a "best friend at work." (Gallup, n.d.). Ultimately, the question implies whether you are connected at work with someone else with whom you can talk, find camaraderie, and enjoy being around. This connection question is a significant indicator of whether someone is engaged in the workplace. To boost morale on the team and prevent burnout, cultivating connections is essential. Hard work becomes more manageable and sometimes exhilarating when one has friends. That's why excellent cultures prioritize intentionally building community within their teams.

One of the best strategies to retain staff members who are aligned with your core values and mission is to find and celebrate the people. Celebrate them frequently. Celebrate not only your friends at work but also those who are contributing to carrying the team forward. The adage, "When you're winning, nothing hurts," rings true. When individuals are celebrated, even the most challenging days become easier to manage. Hope takes root, fueled by the high of being celebrated, filling an individual's emotional reservoir.

CHAPTER 8

~

# Elite Momentum

## Create and Celebrate Momentum

Raise the praise and create a momentum of success. As you experience success, whether big or small, find ways to celebrate it. By doing so, momentum will continue to build, creating an environment filled with accomplishments. Be relentless about positively uplifting others around you and celebrating their achievements, feeding into your culture's momentum. Eventually, you will find yourself in a mode where you can discover celebration in nearly anything, and your environment will be praiseworthy to the point where people feel good about the work they do daily.

> Be relentless about positively uplifting others around you and celebrating their achievements, feeding into your culture's momentum.

## Building and Capitalizing on Momentum

The ability to harness and leverage momentum can differentiate a thriving culture from one that merely survives. Understanding how and when to build and capitalize on momentum is at the heart of success. It recognizes that positive momentum is a byproduct and a driving force that propels everything forward. As positive momentum builds, it becomes a powerful force that is difficult to stop. Collins (2001) describes the impact of tasks such as momentum and how, when you continue to perform them, they begin to have a compound effect on the organization, becoming a powerful force that requires significant effort to halt. Building momentum through recognition, typically tied to success, will compound, having a multifaceted positive impact on the culture. Why positive momentum matters:

1.  Attraction of Good Things:
    *   Positive outcomes attract more positivity. When success becomes a palpable reality, it attracts individuals who wish to contribute and be part of a winning team.

2.  The Irresistible Nature of Success:
    *   People are drawn to success like moths to a flame. When they can see, hear, feel, taste, and even smell success, the desire to gravitate toward it becomes irresistible.

3.  Unstoppable Momentum:
    *   Even when facing challenges, a well-built positive momentum is not easily stopped. While roadblocks may temporarily slow the flywheel, they don't bring it to a halt, especially when the momentum is rapid.

4.  Relentlessness in Promotion:
    *   Building positive momentum is not a passive endeavor. It requires an active and relentless promotion of your mission. As the positive momentum builds, its energy can be harnessed to propel your vision even further.

Recognition of success should be intertwined in everything you do, and the more you do it, the more positive momentum you gain, which is the type of positive cycle any team should want to create.

## Harnessing Positive Momentum in Your Culture

Understanding the psychology behind positive momentum is crucial for building a thriving, positive culture. Much like in sports, celebrating wins can be a game-changer for your staff, students, team, and the overall atmosphere within your school, team, or company. Here's how you can implement a celebration strategy that fosters positive momentum:

1.  Recognizing Wins, Big and Small:
    *   **Strategic pause for adversity:** When facing challenges, take a strategic pause. Acknowledge the adversity and use it as an opportunity to rally the team. This deliberate acknowledgment brings attention to the challenge, making it a focal point for improvement.

        Take a moment to think about a recent struggle. By pausing and reflecting on the challenge, what silver linings have come from it? Maybe it's a new opportunity for clear communication of expectations, recalibrating what is expected. If so, that's still a win arising from a challenge. Positives can be found in just about anything.

        Here's another example: If your data indicates a shortfall, it's crucial to recognize the challenge. Devise a strategic plan, aligning it with your mission to guide everyone collectively toward improvement. Address the areas of concern. When the data shows positive progress in the right direction, it's essential to commemorate the victory. Simple yet powerful, the challenge is addressed, and celebration comes from lifting others up.

- **Quick hits of dopamine:** Celebrate all daily victories. Wins provide a quick hit of dopamine, energizing individuals and teams. Recognize achievements promptly to stimulate a positive rush and reinforce the idea that successes are valued, no matter how small. Stacking small wins creates larger ones!

2. Manufacture Wins:
    - **Seeking solutions:** This strategy is very important, especially if you're just beginning the celebration journey or need a team or individual pick-me-up to manufacture the wins. Actively look for events, big and small, to celebrate. Whether recognizing achievements in academics, extracurricular activities, individual or team accomplishments, or acts of kindness, manufacture wins in any way possible. You must actively look for successes; it's strategic to be proactive instead of waiting for wins to fall in your lap.
    - **Cultural shift:** Consistent celebrations lead to a cultural shift. Your class, school, district, team, and/or business becomes a place where individuals actively contribute to positive momentum, creating a self-sustaining cycle of wins beyond any individual.

Incorporating this celebration strategy into your culture boosts morale and sets the stage for ongoing success. You can create a culture in which positive momentum becomes a way of life by strategically pausing during challenges, celebrating wins promptly, and manufacturing positive events.

## Reinforce and Celebrate Desired Behaviors

Champion the champions! Recognizing and celebrating staff, team members, and students who exemplify the core values of the company, team, or school through their actions is vital in nurturing a thriving culture. Spotlight the desired behavior and contributions to the team. The values we wish to see more of are reinforced, ultimately motivating others to follow a similar path toward excellence.

Returning to the concept of understanding your people's professional love language, speak it in your daily interactions with words of affirmation or provide small tokens of appreciation like handwritten cards. Recognize others for demonstrating excellence in their roles among their peers, as these acts of celebration and appreciation can go a long way in retaining good staff members and creating a dynamic culture. One of the best parts of those tips is that they cost nothing.

Establishing a culture of recognition is essential for fostering a thriving environment. Here are three questions to guide your thoughts on creating your own culture of recognition:

1. How can you champion individuals who consistently embody the core values of your organization through their actions?
2. How can you embrace a culture of appreciation in which every desired action is acknowledged and praised?
3. Considering the concept of professional love languages(Chapman, 1992), how can you speak it in your daily interactions to recognize and celebrate the excellence of your team members?

## Shaping the Narrative: Leveraging Your Online Presence

Education often lags behind other industries in highlighting schools' positive aspects on social media. Fear tends to be one of the predominant factors preventing educators and leaders from sharing the good things happening in classrooms, schools, sports, programs, and extracurricular activities. This fear often stems from concerns about potential negative comments appearing in threads. However, social media platforms offer various features to mitigate the concern, such as turning off comments.

Students and their parents rely on these platforms for school information. Consider the content typically pushed out by school districts to the community—events like lockdowns, responses to lawsuits, or external perspectives shaping narratives. Unfortunately, these tend to be negative in nature and become the sole focus of communication. While such information is undoubtedly important, it should not be the exclusive content shared. If all your audience receives is negative news, that's what they'll come to expect. Proactive cultures nationwide are taking control of their messages, highlighting the positive aspects within their communities and the broader world. Don't succumb to fear; seize control of your narrative and share the uplifting stories within your culture. Be fearless, tell your positive stories, and prevent others from filling a void with their own narratives for personal or political gains.

While the potential for negativity exists, the positives far outweigh the negatives. Promoting the work's good aspects can significantly uplift students, educators, and the school community. It fills student and educator buckets with encouragement and recognition. If you aim to shape the narrative positively, leverage social media. It's a no-cost-effective tool that allows you to build a team to promote the good happening within your educational community collectively. We honor our staff, students, and community by highlighting the good aspects, fortifying morale, and enriching school culture. As simple as it may seem, social media is underutilized in education. There's a reason why thriving businesses and for-profit organizations invest heavily in marketing—it matters. Educators can also harness the power of free media to achieve a similar impact.

In the contemporary landscape of education, it's a common reality for both public and private educational institutions to seek ways to attract more students. Just as businesses actively advertise their services, educational institutions should follow suit. Social media advertising, in particular, offers a unique opportunity for promotional purposes and boosting morale. By showcasing students, staff, schools, and programs, social media becomes a platform to highlight the positive aspects of your educational community. Additionally, it serves as a tool to attract educators who resonate with your mission and witness core values in action. It can be a great hiring tool to attract talent.

Adherence to school, district, local, and state administrative regulations is paramount. It ensures that all communication efforts align with established guidelines and policies, maintaining a professional and compliant environment. These regulations serve as a framework for ethical communication, data privacy, and the overall conduct of educational institutions. By following the guidelines, educators can instill trust and confidence within the community while upholding the standards.

At one high-performing school, they use a helpful strategy for maintaining a steady and sustainable flow of information on social media. Leadership engages the team in a rotational schedule. Team members volunteer for specific days to capture photos, shoot videos, or provide information about noteworthy events or class engagement. This division of responsibilities makes content creation more manageable over time. Additionally, they involve students, especially older ones, like members of the yearbook team, for example, to contribute. They provide educators with content, and they craft the narrative to share on social media.

Naturally, they always adhere to photo or media-sharing guidelines established by the school and district, ensuring that all students have parental permission to be pictured or recorded. They maintain a list of students from the directory of permissions for inclusion in the yearbook and/or on social media. Employing creative techniques, such as capturing the back of heads or using blurred versions, can also be effective. This qualitative approach to sharing positive stories will yield dividends in ways you may not have anticipated. Here are several common social media platforms we can use to shape our narrative:

**YouTube**: Engaging All Audiences

1. **Showcasing Achievements:** Create videos to showcase students' achievements, school events, and notable moments. This provides a dynamic way to celebrate successes and foster a sense of pride.
2. **Storytelling:** Use YouTube to tell compelling stories about the school, its staff, and students. This can include interviews, documentaries, or series that highlight the unique aspects of your class, school, school district, and educational community.

**Instagram**: Connecting with Students and Community

1. **Visual Storytelling:** Leverage Instagram's visual nature for storytelling through images and short videos. This resonates well with students and the broader community.
2. **Student Highlights:** Showcase individual and group achievements, talents, and initiatives. This creates a positive image and inspires other students.
3. **Community Engagement:** Use features like Instagram Stories for real-time updates on events, activities, and important announcements. Encourage interaction through polls and questions.
4. **Behind-the-Scenes:** Provide a behind-the-scenes look at daily school life, classroom activities, and extracurricular events. This personal touch strengthens the connection with the audience.

**Facebook:** Reaching Parents and the Community

1. **Parental Communication:** Establish a consistent communication channel with parents about school activities and important dates/events.
2. **Community Events:** Share information about community events, fundraisers, and partnerships. This helps build positive relationships with the local community.
3. **Visual Updates:** Share photo albums of school events, showcasing the vibrant life within the school. This keeps parents informed and engaged.

**X:** Engaging the Professional and School Community

1. **Professional Learning Network (PLN):** Connect with other educators, administrators, and educational organizations to build a professional learning network. Share insights, resources, and engage in educational discussions.
2. **Quick Updates:** X's concise format is ideal for quick updates, announcements, and sharing links to relevant articles or resources.
3. **Event Promotion:** Effectively promote school events, workshops, and conferences. Using hashtags can amplify the reach of your tweets.
4. **Professional Development Opportunities:** Share information about professional development opportunities, conferences, and workshops. X becomes a real-time source for staying informed about the latest trends in education.

## Creating Compelling Videos

Creating compelling videos for educational purposes using accessible tools like iMovie for Apple iPhones and VideoShow for Android smartphones can be fun and impactful. Here's a guide to help you harness the benefits of these free applications that can easily be attached to the social media outlets available to you:

Benefits of **Using iMovie (free)** (for Apple iPhones):

1. **User-Friendly Interface:** iMovie provides a simple and intuitive interface, making it accessible even for beginners.
2. **Powerful Editing Tools:** It offers a range of editing tools, allowing you to trim, cut, and arrange clips with ease. You can also add music, transitions, and text to enhance your videos.
3. **Templates and Themes:** iMovie has pre-designed templates and themes, making creating professional-looking videos without extensive editing skills convenient.
4. **Seamless Integration:** As an Apple product, iMovie integrates seamlessly with other Apple applications and devices, offering a smooth experience for users in the Apple ecosystem.

**Using VideoShow (free)** on Android Smartphones:

1. **Diverse Editing Tools:** VideoShow on Android offers a variety of editing tools similar to iMovie. You can edit clips, add effects, and incorporate music into your videos.
2. **Multi-Platform Sharing:** VideoShow allows you to share your videos on multiple platforms directly from the app, streamlining the sharing process.
3. **Photo Slideshows:** Besides video editing, VideoShow enables you to create engaging photo slideshows with music, adding

versatility to your content creation.

4. **In-App Effects:** VideoShow provides a range of in-app effects and filters, allowing you to enhance the visual appeal of your videos.

## Tips for Creating Engaging Videos:

1. **B-Roll Footage:** Incorporate B-roll footage to add depth and interest to your videos. B-roll can include supplementary footage or images that support your main content. B-Roll is the fun action clips that glue the video together, keeping the audience engaged.
2. **Best Practices for Holding Your Phone:**
   a. Stability: Hold your phone with both hands to ensure stability and reduce shakiness.
   b. Horizontal Orientation: Record videos in landscape mode for a wider frame which is more suitable for platforms like YouTube.
   c. Vertical Orientation: Recording videos vertically is more suitable for platforms like Instagram and Reels.
3. **Storytelling:** Craft a narrative or storyline to make your videos more engaging and memorable.

By leveraging iMovie and VideoShow's capabilities and following these tips, you can create impactful educational videos that captivate your audience and effectively convey your message.

When creating content, remember to include the links in your staff, class, and parent newsletters for others to access and celebrate what's been spotlighted.

Check out these videos that tell a quick story about the school. Notice how they can be used for school promotion, creating excitement and conveying the narrative the school wants others to see.

## On-Campus Monitors:

Enhancing communication for staff and students through on-campus monitors plays an important role in improving communication within the school community. Here's why educators should leverage on-campus monitors:

1. **Event Promotions:** Display promotions for upcoming events, extracurricular activities, and student achievements. This creates a visually engaging environment within the school.
2. **Weekly Schedules:** Display daily schedules, class changes, and other time-sensitive information. This helps students and staff stay organized.
3. **Visual Recognition:** Celebrate achievements, showcase student work, and recognize staff through visual displays. This fosters a positive and supportive atmosphere on campus.

Students enjoy seeing themselves, friends, and other students in action on the monitors in the school building.

SCAN ME

## CHAPTER 9

~

# Elite Celebration

## Building a Positive School Environment

W hether you walk the halls of an urban school in the United States or a small town in rural America, each institution's unique culture permeates every school entrance, hallway, classroom, and space, leaving an undeniable mark on students and staff alike. Casas (2017), suggests that the undercurrents of our culture don't lie. What stories do the undercurrents at your school say about your culture?

It's easy to fall into the trap of negative thinking, like believing we can't achieve what other schools do because they have resources we don't have. However, we have our own strengths, and our culture can flourish when we focus on our successes and celebrate them. Remember, you can only control what's within your power, so avoid spiraling into negativity by comparing yourself to others. Your environment has the potential to be extraordinary—make it special and unique through your daily actions.

We all have the incredible power to mold the school culture into an environment of positivity, growth, and unity, fostering an atmosphere where success thrives. When this culture extends beyond the school walls, encompassing the entire school community, it brings with it incredible student benefits. Having the right blend of high standards and a positive environment within the school community directly impacts state accountability scores, attendance, and overall morale in the building. Everything done connects to everything else, like a web of positivity linking every aspect together, ultimately leading to student success. Celebrating accomplishments and individuals is one of the most underutilized yet proven strategies to boost morale, staff retention, and overall culture. Celebrate today!

## Celebrate Your Team

As mentioned earlier, celebrate whenever possible. Referring to the same Gallup workplace survey question discussed earlier in the book (Gallup, n.d.), which explores staff engagement, ask yourself, "Over the past seven days, have I received recognition or praise for my commendable work?" Take a moment to reflect on how this question aligns with your experiences over the past work week, considering both those you serve and with whom you collaborate. The ideas may feel small, but in the recognition world, small is big, and big is a significant difference maker. Things that may seem small make a big difference, like celebrating birthdays. When you take action steps towards the celebration goal, you will create a culture in which peer recognition and appreciation are the norm.

## Birthdays!

Who doesn't like to be recognized on their birthday?! As schools or teams expand, departments can take on the responsibility of ensuring that celebrations continue to thrive. For example, an office support team can initiate a simple, yet effective, birthday celebration system. Here's how it works:

1. **Create a Spreadsheet:** Create a shared spreadsheet with columns for names, birthdates, the person's preferences (like their favorite type of cake or treat), and a sign-up section for team members to choose a person to celebrate. By having a sign-up column to choose who will be responsible for organizing the celebration and decor, the burden is lifted off one or a small group of individuals, allowing everyone to have a role and sustaining the celebrating tradition.

2. **Collect Information:** Allow team members to fill in this information as the spreadsheet circulates, or you can gather it from a "family directory," which I'll discuss briefly in the next section.

3. **Plan Celebrations:** When someone's birthday approaches, the individual in charge can schedule a designated time for the team to come together and celebrate. If possible, keep it a surprise; if not, it's still a wonderful opportunity for team bonding, camaraderie, and celebration.

4. **Decorate the Space:** Encourage the person celebrating their birthday to decorate their workspace, classroom, or office. This small effort can make their day more enjoyable and memorable for the entire team. The person responsible for decorating can take it to the next level by staying a bit later the day before or coming in a bit earlier on the celebration day. This way, the celebrated individual enters a fun surprise that will last them all day!

5. **Take the time to celebrate:** During these celebrations, be fully present and engage in non-work-related conversations about the birthday person and each other. It's a time to connect personally, strengthen bonds, and create lasting memories. The short amount of time will go a long way in productivity later. Also, remember that positive culture-building activities like this *are* the work!

These celebrations are a fantastic way to build team spirit, foster positive relationships, and infuse fun into the work environment. Enjoy the process—it's a solid way to strengthen your team while celebrating each other!

## Staff Family Directory

In one school, as part of the onboarding process, new staff members were asked to fill out their own section in the "family directory." The basic information included general details such as their favorite candy, drink, or sweet and a brief blurb about them. This served as another means to foster connections among the staff. When birthdays or "just because" moments arose, fellow staff members could access this information and surprise their colleagues. Ultimately, it was another way of expressing, "You're an integral part of our team, and we see you." This location could also be a great place to include the staff's professional love language.

## Involve Students in Staff Celebrations– The Power of Nominations

I firmly believe that celebrating our dedicated educator staff goes beyond just recognizing their hard work; it's about creating a profound connection between educators and students. One of the most impactful ways to achieve this is by involving students in the staff celebration process, and a powerful strategy for doing this is to encourage students to nominate staff members who exemplify the school's core values. Students can be included in the celebration process by expressing their gratitude through a monthly program allowing them to nominate a teacher who has gone above and beyond to help them. After receiving these nominations, they are gathered and shared directly with the teachers, allowing them to see firsthand their impact on their students' lives. Some students even submit incredibly touching video nominations.

These nominations are like buckets of positivity, filling the hearts of both our staff and students. We also share them in staff meetings, where we lift our teachers up and say, "This is what our students are saying about you." It's a powerful moment when teachers are moved to tears because they hear directly from students.

## Student-Nominated Staff Recognition

1. **Student Empowerment:** By allowing students to nominate staff members, you give them a voice, recognizing educators who make a difference in their lives. They take another level of ownership in their school when they have such a voice.
2. **Alignment with Core Values:** Reinforces the importance of your school's core values and helps students understand how important they are.
3. **Positive School Culture:** Fosters a culture of appreciation and mutual respect between students and staff.

### *How to Implement:*

Begin by promoting the nomination process among students. This can be done through announcements, online educational platforms, or a student voice wall like the one pictured. Provide students with clear guidelines on what makes an educator eligible for nomination. Emphasize the alignment with your school's core values. Encourage students to reflect on how staff members have positively impacted their educational journey, showing them the value of appreciation. This will help educators fill their buckets.

The nomination system could be implemented through written forms, online submissions, or other creative methods, ensuring accessibility to all students. A designated member can review the nominations, ensuring they align with the core values. The information can then recognize and celebrate the nominated staff members. This can be done through awards, certificates, or public acknowledgment during school events or meetings.

### *Impact on School Culture:*

Engaging students in the staff celebration process transforms your school culture into one where appreciation, respect, and recognition are not just words but active principles embraced by all, including the number one stakeholder group—students. By involving students in nominations, you create a cycle of positivity in which staff members feel appreciated, students develop a deeper connection with their educators, and your core values become a living part of your school's identity.

## Students Express Appreciation for the Staff and School

Students can also show their appreciation for the staff and express what they appreciate about the school, and these sentiments can be creatively displayed throughout the school. If you have a theme for the school year, consider encouraging students to write about why they appreciate a teacher, program, or any other positive aspect of the school on a cutout related to that theme (e.g., a bus, graduation hat, or a book for a school-wide book read). Another option could be using hearts during the Valentine's Day season to spread the love.

Engage English teachers in quick-writing activities with these expressions of gratitude, collect them, and then showcase them prominently throughout the school. This initiative will spread gratitude and convey messages of hope, appreciation, and school spirit, fostering a sense of community and connection among students and staff.

## Celebrating Staff Members at Meetings

Another impactful way to celebrate and recognize your dedicated educator staff is by incorporating staff celebrations directly into your regular meetings.

### *Recognizing Staff during Meetings*

Staff meetings are ideal for discussing school matters and uplifting and celebrating educators. By incorporating celebratory elements into meetings, you can reinforce the idea that your staff is at the heart of your school's success. During staff meetings, take the opportunity to recognize and appreciate the hard work of specific staff members who have gone above and beyond. This can be done by presenting them with personalized banners that showcase their name, title, and the number of years they've dedicated to the school. Such banners serve as a tangible symbol of appreciation that educators can proudly display.

### *Here's how you can extend the celebration:*

As we discussed before, take all the wins to social media. Celebrating your staff during meetings need not be confined to the meeting room alone. It can extend to a broader audience through various online platforms. Extending the story beyond your walls allows others to join in and contribute, fostering connections, especially when celebrating the staff. It also allows the recognition received by the staff member to be lifted high, reaching the school community and expanding in ways that go beyond local proximity.

Document these moments by taking photos or short videos of staff members receiving their banners and being celebrated. Share these highlights on your school's social media channels. Don't forget to send the recipient these pictures and/or videos. They will turn around and upload them for their social community to see and share in the celebration. This, in turn, promotes both them and the school, recognizing their achievements. It paints a positive picture for all.

## Take Celebrating to the Next Level

Celebrating dedicated educators during meetings is a powerful strategy, but let's take it to the next level. Here's how you can elevate staff recognition and take it further:

Once the personalized banner or certificate arrives or is completed, don't stop at handing it over during the meeting. Instead, celebrate with a certificate at the staff meeting and organize a classroom celebration. The certificate and/or token are one element during the staff meeting, but the second is the classroom celebration.

Invite a group of enthusiastic students to be part of this special moment. This can include your leadership classes or willing classes and teachers to help celebrate the educator. Their involvement adds an extra layer of warmth and authenticity to the celebration. Accompanied by these students, take the banner and/or certificate to the honored staff member's classroom during a class session and cheer for the teacher.

Have a designee record this memorable occasion on video. As previously discussed, this preserves the moment for the educator and creates content that can be shared with the greater school community and beyond.

Another factor that a banner/certificate allows for is the opportunity to display educator recognitions inside or outside their area proudly. Many staff members will proudly display their banners. This will remind them of the appreciation and serve as an example to students and others who enter their classrooms. You will begin to see staff framing and showcasing their certificates and banners in their rooms and on their personal social media. Don't forget to include a link to the video in the staff and parents' newsletters so that the school community can enjoy participating in the celebration. School and personal pride will accompany their recognition, directly reinvesting into the culture.

# CHAPTER 10

~

# Elite Community

## We Don't Enroll Students; We Enroll Families

Hamish Brewer, a notable educational leader and speaker, understood that one key to his team's success was recruiting families to participate in the entire school community process (Brewer, 2019). Hamish, often called the "Skateboarding Principal," gained recognition for his unconventional and energetic approach to school leadership, creating a positive and dynamic school culture. He stresses the importance of family engagement and says, "We don't enroll students; we enroll families" in his school setting, contributing significantly to the elite school cultures he led as a principal (Brewer, 2019). He understood the importance of the whole school community and the impact that it can have on an entire school culture.

Building a strong partnership with parents is a cornerstone of educational success. Parents entrust their children to schools, expecting academic guidance and a positive impact on their lives. This responsibility signals the importance of teachers, support staff, and educators' work in their roles in education. When educators and parents form a collaborative partnership, the combined effort becomes a powerful force for the student's benefit. The alignment of care and interest between the home and school sends a powerful message to the student.

Extensive research found in organizational work such as the National PTA at pta.org (National PTA, n.d.) consistently demonstrates that when families actively participate in their children's education, it significantly improves student success. Engaged families contribute to higher graduation rates, improved academic performance, enhanced attendance records, and increased likelihood of pursuing higher education and technical schools. Beyond academics, parental involvement also notably affects students' social and emotional well-being. According to an American Psychological Association (APA) study (American Psychological Association [APA], n.d.), not only does such involvement correlate with better academic outcomes, but it also positively influences students' social and emotional skills while reducing instances of delinquency.

### *Benefits at a Glance:*

According to research by the National PTA at pta.org (National PTA, n.d.), family involvement has many benefits. Here are some at a glance.

**Academic Success**: Students generally perform better academically when their families actively participate in their education. This involvement includes assisting with homework, attending school events, and engaging in parent-teacher conferences.

**Improved Behavior**: Children whose parents actively participate in their school tend to display better behavior and experience fewer disciplinary issues. This positive trend may stem from the sense of support and accountability associated with parental engagement.

**Higher Attendance**: Schools frequently report increased attendance rates when parents are actively engaged. Parents involved in their child's education are more likely to prioritize regular school attendance.

**Enhanced Social Skills**: Students with engaged parents often develop stronger social skills and are more prone to positive peer interactions.

**Increased Motivation and Interest in Learning**: Parental involvement can positively impact a child's attitude toward learning. When parents express interest in their child's education, it can inspire the child to be more engaged and enthusiastic about learning.

**Positive Attitude Toward School**: Children with involved parents are likely to cultivate a positive attitude toward school. They perceive education as valuable and important when their families actively provide support.

## From Tragedy to Triumph; Being Connected at School: Scott's Story

*My name is Scott Payne. I am a 43-year-old father of two incredible middle school children, and this is my story. It's a tale of loss, resilience, and the power of a simple smile to transform a moment, a day, or even a life. My journey into fatherhood and community leadership is deeply intertwined with a personal tragedy that shaped my outlook on life and my mission to make a difference in my community.*

*When I was nine, my world was turned upside down. My father, a man I looked up to and loved dearly for the short nine years I knew him, made the very unfortunate decision to take his* own life after an extreme battle with depression following a difficult divorce from my mother. My last memory of him is a seemingly ordinary morning drop-off at my elementary school. I got out of the car and said goodbye, not knowing it would be the last time I would see him. I have very few memories as a kid, but that one moment has stayed with me—a constant reminder of how quickly things can change and the importance of cherishing every second we have with our loved ones.

This profound loss has fueled a passion within me to ensure that no child feels alone or without support. It's why I've dedicated myself to being active in my kids' school community, mainly through the Dad's Club at their schools. Traditionally, involvement like this might taper off after elementary school, but I saw an opportunity to extend its positive impact. I championed that our presence and engagement could be just as transformative for middle schoolers navigating one of the most challenging phases of their young lives.

Some middle schools have Dads' Clubs or Dads in the PTA who help teachers and staff occasionally with various campus events throughout the school year. Our middle school had this in the years before my kids came. But when my kids came to the school, I approached the principal with the idea of having the Dads' Club open doors for the kids every morning, just as we did at our elementary school, and he welcomed the idea with open arms. Not only that, but we've partnered to strategize ways to keep our students safe and parents alert during the early morning dropoff, which gets our students into the classrooms as early as possible and keeps our teachers ready to rock and roll to start their days!

The dads do more than just open car doors at drop-off. We're there to offer a smile, a high five, or a word of encouragement. We aim to be a positive force, a beacon of light on good and bad days. And yes, I'm that dad—Mr. Payne—who might just be wearing a ridiculous wig or breaking into dance as you walk by. Why?

*Because if I can make even one child laugh or momentarily forget their troubles, I've done my job.*

*This role has become my way of giving back, building, and strengthening the bonds between fathers and their children. It's a testament to the belief that something as simple as being present and offering a moment of joy can leave a lasting impression. My father's absence taught me the importance of these connections, and I strive to fill the lives of not only my children but all those in our school community with the presence, laughter, and love that I missed growing up without a dad in my life.*

*We've created a space where fathers can come together to support their kids and every child who walks through the school doors. It's a commitment to being there, showing up, and making a difference one smile at a time. This is my story of turning personal tragedy into a force for good, transforming pain into purpose. And as long as I can, I'll continue to don those wigs, dance those dances, and open those car doors, hoping to make the world a little brighter for someone else.*

Scott Payne-Dads Club, President

## Build a Powerful School Community Team

Like Scott, everyone has the potential to have a major impact on those around them when they choose to embrace that role. This belief extends to the school community beyond the walls of a school. An example of such impact can be found at any local school through the volunteers and members of a school's Parent Teacher Association/Organization (PTA/O), Parent Teacher Student Association/Organization (PTSA/O), or any other organization that brings the school community together. Here is a breakdown of how the partnership can flourish to create an elite environment.

+ **Parents** (PTSA): One of the building blocks of a strong foundation is a close-knit community, and our Parent Teacher Student Association (PTSA) is at the heart of it. A school's PTSA can be pivotal in coordinating social events like school dances and actively supporting various extracurricular booster clubs, all while ensuring student and staff celebrations are vibrant and meaningful. Parents help encourage, support, and can feed the staff, creating appreciation for the building's hard-working teachers, support staff, and educators. Partnering with your PTSA keeps the staff focused on teaching, learning, and relationships.

+ **Teachers** (PTSA): Teachers also benefit from a strong parent-teacher relationship regarding encouragement. Partner with your PTSA to support teachers throughout the school year by providing words of affirmation and small tangible tokens of appreciation. These are key to a healthy school staff environment and assist in retention. When teachers feel valued, there is less opportunity for burnout to set in. Teachers, in turn, show their appreciation for the important work parents do to invest in the students.

+ **Student** (PTSA): Students are also integral leaders in the school community. They advocate for meaningful causes, participate in meetings, and contribute to planning various charitable initiatives throughout the school year. Examples include students helping lead charitable, social awareness, and or culture-building events. Elite cultures enable students to collaborate with the school and organization, empowering them to take on leadership roles.

+ **Association** should include the whole **school community** (PTSA): Partnership with local charities makes a meaningful difference in the school experience. With this partnership, you can help provide essential items, food, toys, and support to children and families in need, especially during the holiday season, including the students in need at the school, which can be done confidentially through adults (e.g., counselors at school).

These initiatives are just some ways the school community leads on and beyond the campus, fostering a culture of learning, well-being, service to others, and community engagement.

It's worth emphasizing that when students' families are welcomed into the school setting, everything typically improves for the student, including attendance, engagement, grades, and behavior. Embracing family involvement is one of the essential "tier 1" principles for student engagement. Even if a student's family members cannot actively participate, the presence of other involved adults still positively contributes to other students and the school environment. This might require a mindset shift for some educators, but it creates a win-win scenario for those who embrace family participation, benefiting everyone.

## The Impact of Dads Club on School Community and Safety

The Dads Club is an extension of the PTA, adding another elite dimension to any school. The involvement of dads contributes to a better overall school environment and enhanced student achievement, supported by research-backed statistics (National PTA, n.d.). As an additional arm of the PTA, the Dads Club brings various elements, including a physical presence, that fosters an increased sense of safety for students and parents. They contribute to a thriving culture on campus by greeting students in the morning, accompanied by uplifting music during car drop-off. Dads play a vital role in supporting various school causes and assisting students in giving back to the community.

For instance, they collaborate with school administration and can help connect local safety departments like the police or fire departments to promote a broader sense of school community. The involvement of police department members establishes a shared partnership, creating a safe and secure atmosphere while embodying the community-policing aspect that police departments aim for. This collaboration pays dividends for both the school and the community.

## Partners Beyond the School Walls: Community Fire and Policing Practices

In most places in our country, the school community surrounding the physical location of the campus eagerly wants to be a part of the school. A strong school community is good for the area, businesses, and the overall well-being of the people within the school community. Schools need partners to help build a thriving community.

Businesses should proudly partner with their surrounding schools; it's good for business and your organization. How can you connect? Consider offering morale-boosting treats and small gestures to help the staff feel valued throughout the school year. This direct impact on the staff indirectly extends to the students, contributing to the positive environment it helps create.

At one school, the city and city council members actively engaged with the school, showcasing a strong partnership. The police department played a significant role in establishing a positive police presence and exemplifying community policing practices. The fire department routinely contributed by providing their fire truck for fundraisers, such as helping acquire turkeys around Thanksgiving in partnership with student leadership groups, to give back to those in need in and around the school community. Their involvement helped raise awareness for charitable events organized by the school. This elite school community culture didn't emerge out of thin air; instead, it was cultivated through intentional partnerships forged by educators on campus and the school community.

## Beyond the Badge: Chief Miller's Elite Culture and School Partnership

In the heart of Colleyville, Texas, Police Chief Michael Miller is a beacon of leadership, embodying the principles of an elite culture within the police department. His commitment to high standards and positive community policing has transformed the department into a symbol of resilience and collaboration. Beyond enforcing the law, Chief Miller has forged intentional relationships with the local school community, creating a partnership that would prove crucial in an internationally publicized event.

The Chief found himself thrust into the international spotlight when a terrorist took four hostages in a local synagogue. The SWAT team and negotiators grappled with the unfolding situation for eleven intense hours on a windy Saturday. Over 250 law enforcement agents, including the FBI and other state and national agencies, converged on the city to resolve the crisis. Interestingly, these very campuses were where city officers would high-five and fist-bump students during drop-offs. Multiple school campuses were their main stationing areas during the fateful weekend event.

As events unfolded, the schools became a central hub for various emergency agencies. It was another reason for such a strong partnership with the school community and stakeholders. The event had a profound impact as images of the school appeared on TV. The familiarity of the schools being used to house the various agencies involved, including the SWAT team and other first responders, hit home. Fortunately, the efforts of the negotiators and an elite hostage rescue team from Quantico, Virginia, led to a successful resolution. The rescue team neutralized the terrorists and freed the hostages.

The experience underscored the importance of intentional relationships within a community. Chief Miller's leadership exemplified the importance of fostering a positive police culture. The community-policing initiatives further underscored this commitment. These efforts high-lighted the value of maintaining high standards in task execution. Additionally, they emphasized the importance of positive community building. The impact extended beyond the organization itself. Partner-ships matter. It impacts everything in a way that affects every individual around.

## Launching Success: Engaging Families

At the beginning of the school year, everyone can engage families. Conducting a starting-of-the-year meeting with all families provides a platform to communicate expectations for the academic year, including aspects like attendance, processes, and more. Additionally, it serves as an opportunity to enlist the school community's involvement, whether through their time, financial contributions, or general support for the school. Elite cultures for participation and communication initiate this process early, before students arrive, possibly in spring, addressing scheduling and other essential information before the upcoming school year. For some, this early engagement involves helping students plan for success in the forthcoming academic year and providing information regarding their schedules and courses that pique students' interest.

## First Impression: Late Winter Event

As described, early meetings are crucial in familiarizing future families with their new school. These meetings provide an opportunity to ask initial questions and initiate rapport with the staff. Ideally, this late winter parent and student information event should commence as early as February/March before the next school year begins. This event is designed for the incoming class for the next school year who are new to your school. It's the first impression you make. For secondary schools, the event is when students, with the help of their families, embark on making course selections and witness the showcase of elective options. It is an opportunity for your new families to reduce their stress and anxiety about the upcoming school year. Follow these steps to make the event successful:

1. Choose the best date possible in late winter.
2. Organize your team efficiently, covering all event details.
3. Promote the event through your weekly newsletter and social media, and coordinate with feeder schools for mutual promotion.
4. Craft a concise message, highlighting crucial information such as class selection for scheduling.
5. Develop a plan with your team for final details, including attire and handouts.
6. During the event, it's showtime. This initial interaction is your chance to make a lasting impression. Infuse your core values to

showcase your standards and immerse families in the culture you uphold.

## Second First Impression: Back-to-School Camp and Orientation

The second opportunity for a pre-school-year meeting, scheduled just before the start of the new school year, aims to engage students and families before the first day of school. This is another chance to put your team's best foot forward, creating momentum for the upcoming school year. It's the perfect occasion to discuss the standards and culture of the school community, guiding how everyone can appropriately engage with one another. This simultaneous conversation establishes a mutual space for trust and a shared partnership between the school and families. As parents receive essential information for a successful start to the school year and are encouraged to partner with the school, students undergo their own version of a camp in a different part of the building. This simulation provides insights into what a school day will look like, with teams navigating a modified mock schedule, learning the layout of the school building, understanding expectations for class and hallway behavior, receiving cafeteria instructions, and gaining other day-to-day advice from staff and student leaders. This comprehensive event sets the tone for specific orientations tailored to families and students. Following this experience, students feel less stressed about the first day of school and are equipped with a good understanding of where to go and what to do. Parents, too, experience reduced stress, having learned the daily routines of drop-off and pick-up and how to contact individuals if needed. This pivotal event establishes a positive tone for the entire school year.

## Building Strong Partnerships: Gaining PTA Buy-In for School Success

Each community has distinct needs, and the more educators can tap into parental and community support, the more opportunities arise for staff, including teachers, to concentrate on building relationships and focusing on academics. Increased external support translates to more time and resources for staff and teachers.

Examples of activities that can occur during the school day or after hours include "Coffee with the Principal," which provides an opportunity to showcase different aspects of the school, connect with the community, and address any questions or disseminate important information. Following these meetings, the PTA can conduct their required meetings and explore additional ways to connect with the school and staff.

The PTA can play a vital role in providing various meals for the staff, including breakfasts, lunches, and dinners before evening campus-wide events. Additionally, they can contribute to communication efforts across various social media platforms, helping to share the desired narrative within the school community. The PTA can also actively support leading fundraising initiatives, such as spirit nights and booster clubs.

In terms of events, the PTA can play a role in organizing a lively back-to-school social featuring inflatables, a dunk tank, music, food, snacks, and various sports activities on the field. Optimal attendance is achieved by scheduling the event right after school on a Friday. Organizing events that students are eager to participate in—especially on days like Fridays or before major holidays—optimizes overall attendance at school and the event. This consideration is crucial for overall school accountability measures and contributes significantly to positive culture-building efforts—details like date and time placement matter. By having an event directly after school, students can join in immediately after their last class without the need to go home first. Additionally, this timing allows staff members to be present and eliminates the long nights for staff and students who have already experienced a full school day.

PTAs can assist by supporting students in financial need and working closely with the counseling and administration team to ensure confidentiality that would remain on the school side, an extremely important aspect of the scholarship.

## Fundraising and Family Programs

The PTA can also support the school through creative fundraising initiatives. One such initiative involves candy grams, which can be integral to their fundraising efforts. These grams are sold at school, communicated through parent newsletters or events, and distributed by dedicated parent volunteers during school lunches. Examples of candy grams include "smartie" grams, where parents can write encouraging notes delivered to students during the first week of school. Other candy grams can be themed, such as "boo" grams for Halloween, "Valentine" grams, and "candy cane" grams during the holiday season. Through these fundraising events, the PTA not only raises funds but also organizes and distributes items, allowing the staff to focus on the overall well-being and behavior of the students.

In addition to fundraising, PTAs contribute to family programs by organizing information nights on various topics. For instance, "Tech talks" can address hot topics for parents, providing insights into technology use and highlighting potentially dangerous apps on phones and other devices. This proactive approach helps parents stay informed and vigilant.

Furthermore, PTAs can help take the lead in organizing standard dance nights, enhancing the social and recreational aspects of the school community. Allowing the PTA to lead in this initiative relieves educators on campus from an additional responsibility amidst their already full plates. The PTA adopts a divide-and-conquer approach, leveraging the passions and interests of volunteers to distribute responsibilities throughout the school year.

This strategy ensures that the same individuals are not shouldering the entire burden, aligning with the principle that everyone possesses unique strengths and passions. By capitalizing on these strengths, individuals can contribute meaningfully—whether it's expertise in balloon archways, DJ skills, catering, creativity, decorations, and more. This approach taps into the diverse strengths of the school community.

## Uniting Students and Community for Meaningful Impact

As integral leaders in the community, students actively champion meaningful causes, fostering a sense of citizenship within the school. They participate in meetings and are crucial in planning various charitable initiatives throughout the school year. By partnering with the community, students can elevate events to new heights.

For example, at one school, students organize their traditional annual "Color Run," inspired by a fellow student's battle with cancer.

Collaborating with student organizations, the PTA, and the school community, they themed a September pep rally during Childhood Cancer Awareness Month to raise awareness. They collectively raised over $9,000 to support the child battling cancer and his family. Beyond the Color Run, students lead impactful charity fundraisers in collaboration with the community, such as Pasta for Pennies, benefiting leukemia, lymphoma, and myeloma patients, and Soles4Souls, collecting hundreds of shoes for those in need worldwide. The partnership with the local charity GRACE empowers them to make a meaningful difference, providing essential items, food, toys, and support to children and families in need, particularly during the holiday season.

## Delightful Moments: PTA's Themed Days for Boosting Staff Morale

For staff morale, the PTA can organize themed days to boost spirits. These include a coffee bar, sundae bars featuring a plethora of toppings from candies to syrups, a trail mix bar, a hot cocoa and candy bar, a popcorn bar with assorted treats and refreshments, and a fall-themed bar with cookies, pumpkin cakes, pumpkin spice lattes, and other autumn delights. These initiatives aim to provide enjoyable and uplifting moments for educators.

If the leadership team, a specific department, or a sunshine committee would like to take the lead, they can go beyond the PTA or in addition to it. Consider trolley carts with treats and tokens of appreciation during various holidays or whenever the campus's pulse needs a boost. As an educator, it is important to have a pulse on students and staff.

Opening Day for baseball is a great season to have a hotdog bar with all the sides and festive decor. If the weather is cold, it sounds like it's time for a chili cookoff by the staff, accompanied by a fun prize that can be a made-up trophy or even a simple gift card. How about "Super Bowl" Sunday Soup? The Friday before the Super Bowl is a perfect time to get festive and have a soup bar with all the sides brought by the team. Simply find moments and reasons to have fun. These are simple ways to boost morale and build team camaraderie. By boosting morale, you enhance emotional capacity, directly impacting everyone's well-being and enabling them to perform their roles even more effectively.

## Combining PTA and Dads Club–Extended Lunch Wellness Extravaganza

The concept of extended lunch is a powerful tool that can also foster a vibrant and connected school community. Imagine adding an extra refreshing 15-20 minutes to lunchtime, allowing educators to unwind and share moments of camaraderie. This simple adjustment creates a breathing space for teachers and lays the foundation for a positive and collaborative community atmosphere. As the team schedules these extended lunch days, thoughtful consideration is given to weather conditions, ensuring the outdoor setting enhances the experience.

The extended lunch moments are more than just an elongated break—they can also be a celebration of the school community. Picture the scene: the PTA and Dad's club actively contributing to the occasion, firing up grills with sizzling burgers and hotdogs, setting the stage for a lively gathering. With music in the background, staff members engage in light-hearted conversations, fostering connections beyond the confines of the classroom. The Dad's Club and PTA, crucial support pillars, play a hands-on role in event logistics, from setup to teardown, reinforcing their connection with the staff.

Simultaneously, the broader community, represented by the PTA and general school community, including health businesses, seize the opportunity to engage with students through a dynamic wellness day while the extended lunch is happening. While educators enjoy an extended lunchtime with good food, music, and camaraderie, students are outdoors enjoying the fresh air and getting some natural vitamin D from the sun. This initiative offers various activities, creating a festive atmosphere that resonates throughout the school. Beyond the joyous interactions, this extended lunch strategy aligns with a broader goal—the positive school culture radiates outward, enveloping the entire school community. This interconnectedness amplifies school pride, fostering an environment where students, staff, and the school community thrive together, with the ultimate beneficiary being the students.

Picture a vibrant scene where a volunteer takes on the role of a DJ, infusing the atmosphere with lively tunes, setting the stage for an energetic student gathering while staff members enjoy their extended lunch. Volunteers at wellness stations strategically placed across the grounds oversee various activities—races, throwing competitions, jump ropes, heavy ropes, sports games, and more. It's a holistic approach to wellness and enjoyment, creating an experience that resonates with students and adults alike.

While the students revel in their activities, the adults, including educators and volunteers, enjoy camaraderie and shared experiences. Behind the scenes, meticulous organization ensures seamless supervision and efficient time rotation, underscoring the importance of logistics in making these events a success. Though significant, the effort invested in this behind-the-scenes work by your team and volunteers pales compared to the substantial benefits of nurturing a positive environment.

Want to elevate it another notch? Consider acquiring some form of transportation, such as a golf cart, to shuttle the teachers between the designated area and the school building, especially if there is some distance between the two locations.

The ripple effects of these events extend far beyond the immediate participants. Building a positive environment becomes a shared endeavor involving staff, students, and the broader school community. Partnerships between students, staff, parents, and the community take root and flourish, creating an environment aligned with the desired values of the school community. It's a symbiotic relationship—a genuine win-win for everyone involved. The time investment pays off through heightened morale, strengthened bonds, and a shared commitment to fostering a positive and thriving educational community.

Here is an example schedule of the extended lunch concept, provided for everyone by adding fifteen minutes to the lunch schedule. The regular lunch schedule might look like this:

A - 11:30-12:00
B - 12:00-12:30
C - 12:30-1:00

The extended lunch schedule will be adjusted as follows:

A - 11:30-12:15
B - 11:45-12:30
C - 12:15-1:00

When there is an overlap in lunch periods, such as between A lunch at 11:45 and B lunch at 12:15, students from the previous lunch (A) proceed to the designated location for activities before the B lunch students arrive. Ideally, this is a large field separate from the eating location. When students go to their designated areas, it will allow the cleanup crew to perform their regular cleaning tasks before the next group enters the cafeteria, and this process is repeated for however many lunches you may have. Naturally, picking a time of year when the weather is typically pleasant is best.

Even if the students don't have all the extra activities, they would still appreciate the additional time to soak in some Vitamin D and just be kids—playing, reading, walking, or talking. Have some soccer or footballs nearby and watch the play unfold.

The time together fosters the desire to be one big team working toward the same mission: creating a positive environment for students to learn and grow. The community enjoys offering this time for staff, and students reap the benefits of increased movement and additional time to spend with friends or engage in physical activities. This is yet another event that can dangle like a carrot for students, ensuring that their behavior meets the expectations inside the school building, incentivizing yet another event they would not want to miss.

## Building an Elite Culture: One Step at a Time

Do you remember towards the beginning of the book when I said that I would repeat the importance of taking on these strategies one step at a time? Well, here it is. This all takes time, so do it one step at a time. Remember, all these events, strategies, and ideas take time. Realistically, it is overwhelming if none of these things are currently in place. You must allow yourself to tackle this large elephant one bite at a time. These elite events don't just happen overnight. Like anything else done at a high level, time in daily, weekly, monthly, and annual year-after-year school life is a requirement. Choose one thing and focus on how to develop it over time. Then, choose the next thing when the first becomes part of the normal day-to-day, and so on.

# CHAPTER 11

~

# Elite Engagement

## Create Spaces of High Engagement

Learning thrives when it becomes an enthralling adventure. Students crave engagement. Students are wired to seek engagement in today's digital age, where social media and smartphones dominate. It may be challenging for those outside of the current school-age generation to accept it entirely, but this is the reality we face. So, the question arises: How are you effectively engaging your students? The second question is whether you aim for engaged students or simply compliant students. It's important to recognize that there is a distinction between the two.

Establishing a classroom or school that genuinely engages students requires prioritizing activities, lessons, and extracurriculars that spark their passion for knowledge and exploration. Empowering students to participate in their learning journey actively boosts their enthusiasm and fosters a lifelong love for learning.

Implementing effective teaching practices such as AVID (Advancement Via Individual Determination, n.d.), Kagan strategies (Kagan & Kagan, 2009), and student-centered approaches incorporating cutting-edge technology interactions, including the latest advancements in AI and augmented reality, can help cultivate a dynamic learning environment. This, in turn, directly contributes to improved student attendance, morale, and engagement.

Creating an engaging learning environment isn't something one can grasp through osmosis. It requires intentional effort and continuous improvement. Here are some questions to help sharpen your skills as you embark on this journey:

1. Do you desire to learn and enhance your teaching practice? If you're reading this, the answer is likely yes—great!
2. Do you have a clear focus, or do you need to choose one strategy from those mentioned? Start by learning about that strategy and how to apply it in your learning environment. In the next section, I'll also show you how to harness key elements that make learning environments highly engaging and elite.
3. Implement what you've learned to enhance your engaging environment, refine your approach, apply your newfound knowledge, and repeat the process.

Creating an engaging classroom is an ongoing journey, and these steps will help you get started and continually improve your teaching methods.

## Elements of an Engaging Lesson Framework

Engagement serves as a cornerstone for creating an energetic and dynamic classroom environment. As educators, here's a guide to enhancing classroom engagement:

1. Anticipation and Excitement:
    + Before class: Reflect on how your students feel heading to your class. Are they excited, anticipating the upcoming lesson?

- Class design: What does your classroom look like? Is it inviting or stale?
- Upon entry: Create an inviting atmosphere as students enter. Greet them personally, making them feel known and valued.

2. Welcoming Environment:
   - Personalized greetings: Greet students by name at the door. Personal connections foster a sense of belonging.
   - Visibility: Ensure students see you as approachable and ready to guide and support them.

3. Engaging Introductions:
   - Music or video hook: Set the tone with enticing music or video to capture their attention and build anticipation for the day's learning.
   - Clear expectations: Communicate expectations for classroom routines and procedures. Clarity promotes a sense of security. When students know what to expect, they have the framework to work safely within those boundaries.

4. Passion for Teaching:
   - Infuse passion: Share your passion for the subject matter. Enthusiasm is contagious, and it fosters a positive attitude toward learning.
   - Connect regardless of topic: Your passion can bridge gaps and engage students even in challenging topics.

5. Interactive Learning:
   - Articulation opportunities: Provide opportunities for students to articulate what they're learning. This aids in processing, understanding, and retaining information. Proven, yet simple, strategies like "turn and talk" help students connect and facilitate better processing and retention of information.

+ Student participation: Encourage active participation during lessons. Create an environment in which students feel comfortable expressing their thoughts.

6. Reflection and Retention:

   + Reflective practices: Implement opportunities for students to reflect on their learning. This can be through discussions, journaling, or other reflective exercises.

   + Spiraled learning: Integrate a review or warm-up activity related to previous learning. This boosts retention when information is spiraled into the following day's lessons. This can happen anywhere within your lesson.

7. Closure and Wrap-Up:

   + Bow tie on the learning: Conclude each class period with a summary or wrap-up activity. This helps solidify the day's learning and provides closure.

   + Reflection opportunities: Allow time for students to reflect on what they've learned. This reflection supports deeper understanding and retention.

Remember, the key is to create a classroom environment in which students feel educated, inspired, and excited about learning. By incorporating these practices, you build a vibrant and engaging educational experience.

## Backward Design

Don't overlook the significance of backward design when establishing your organization's goals. Once your goals are identified, employ a backward design approach to delineate the milestones that will guide your journey toward achieving these goals throughout the year. For educators, especially if excelling in state accountability tests is a goal, deliberate planning and allocating sufficient time for teaching and learning become paramount. Here are some details for both school leaders and teachers to consider:

1. **Calendar planning:** For example, identify the date of your state assessment and mark it on your calendar. Utilize backward design to structure the learning phases in a manageable time, ensuring a steady progression. Avoid the common pitfall of feeling rushed or running out of time.

2. **Realistic time frames:** Create realistic time frames for holidays, pep rallies, and mandatory drills. Allocate space within your timeline for unforeseen events that inevitably arise during the school year, such as required programs or practices mandated by your school, local authorities, or the state.

3. **Attention to detail:** Elite classes thrive on meticulous planning that considers all details. Assess whether your planning accommodates day-to-day intricacies and time constraints. Consider factors like programs requiring student participation and whether your district and school leaders provide plans that adequately address these details. If not, plan for them.

## The Strategic Benefits of School-Year Themes

Crafting a thematic focus for the school year that aligns with the overall mission and core values is a strategic initiative that reaps numerous benefits. Choosing themes in harmony with best practices in professional development ensures a cohesive and purposeful approach to growth for staff and students.

A themed approach can also be extended to commemorate significant milestones, with leadership and/or PTA playing a pivotal role in creating a festive and memorable atmosphere throughout the school year. Notably, the chosen theme becomes a unifying thread woven throughout the school year, creating a shared narrative, behind which everyone can rally.

The theme's visibility can be heightened through the strategic use of social media, utilizing a dedicated hashtag. This tracks the theme's progression and serves as a platform to showcase and celebrate the diverse range of activities and achievements—significant and small— that contribute to the school's overarching mission. This deliberate thematic approach helps maintain focus on the chosen aspects, whether it's upholding high expectations and standards or fostering a positive environment, fostering a sense of unity and purpose within the school community.

Below are some impactful books; each can be paired with a theme that can elevate any school year by fostering embedded learning, building a positive environment, and providing strategies and ideas. Coupling these resources with a focused theme throughout the year can solidify student and staff messages and aspirations.

### The Energy Bus for Schools: Positive Culture Building

Embracing the "Energy Bus" theme aligns with a book study on *The Energy Bus for Schools* (Gordon and Van Allan, 2024). This book offers an excellent foundation for a theme centered around uniting the entire team—a district, school, class, or any other type of team—towards a common goal of positivity. The associated *Energy Bus for Schools* program (Gordon and Van Allan, 2024) further enhances the theme, providing valuable resources, a character and leadership curriculum, and consistent communication throughout the school year.

### Teach Like a Pirate: Engaging Classrooms

Adopting a pirate theme for a book study on *Teach Like a Pirate* (Burgess, 2012) is another impactful choice. This book study has the potential to elevate engagement levels throughout the entire school by infusing a lively pirate theme into various aspects of the academic year while focusing on overall student and staff engagement.

### Culturize: Building Relationships and Elevating Excellence

Explore *Culturize* (Casas, 2017) for valuable insights on fostering a community of learners. The theme emphasizes cultivating innate human traits such as kindness, honesty, and compassion, which are crucial for students and staff. Adopting the principles from *Culturize* and creating a theme will significantly contribute to relationship building and overall excellence within the school community.

### The Power of a Positive Team: Team Positivity

Dive into *The Power of a Positive Team* (Gordon, 2018) to inspire a theme that aligns with a book study. Consider integrating school colors, especially adding a touch of blue (book cover color), to synchronize with the book's essence. This approach ensures a focused exploration of pertinent subjects, and when tailored to align with the school or district's focus areas, the theme becomes even more impactful and relevant.

## Empowering Educators for Student Success

Educational leaders, I have a question for you. How can we tap into a teacher's drive to enhance their professional skills and empower our veteran educators to excel and indulge their curiosities through ongoing development? The answer lies in creating a dynamic learning atmosphere that profoundly impacts student attendance and enthusiasm.

When students develop a genuine eagerness to actively participate in class and feel a heightened sense of belonging, their motivation to attend school naturally intensifies. This, in turn, leads to improved attendance rates, enhanced academic achievements, and an overall boost in student well-being.

It's worth noting that excellent educators are inherently motivated to learn and refine their craft to improve their students and the learning environment. Professional development opportunities that are meaningful, purposeful, and tailored to educators' specific classroom needs are very important to their level of engagement.

Are there veteran and or high-achieving teachers within your organization who excel in specific areas of classroom management, instruction, fostering class culture, implementing routines, or establishing procedures? If so, how are you harnessing their expertise to serve as models for their peers? Here are several ways for your teacher leaders to contribute and be recognized as exemplary models, elevating their status and bringing them into the overall culture even more:

1. **Professional development rotations:** During scheduled professional development sessions, organize rotations of mini-sessions facilitated by willing teacher-leaders. Arrange for groups of teachers to rotate through these sessions based on their specific needs. Teachers often appreciate learning from their colleagues who have proven success in specific areas.

2. **Staff meeting mini-sessions:** Incorporate short, focused mini-sessions led by experienced educators during staff meetings. This allows for sharing best practices and insights within a manageable timeframe.

3. **Utilize Professional Learning Communities (PLCs):** Use your PLC time effectively by including structured learning sessions. An actual PLC should be a collaborative learning and growth platform, with opportunities for teachers to learn from and contribute to the collective knowledge.

By embracing these strategies, you can tap into the expertise of your teacher leaders, promote a culture of shared learning, and foster an environment in which educators continually support and elevate one another. This benefits teachers and enhances the overall educational experience for students. More tools for your toolbox:

Ask yourself the following questions:

1. Are students engaged, compliant, or off-task? The answer often lies in the culture of that classroom, which extends to the overall school environment.
2. Are students excited to come to school? What do they look forward to? What motivates them to want to be there? Create engagement in every way possible, and you will see the positive benefits of your efforts.
3. What do your pep rallies and student events look like? Do you have them? If so, what do your students say about them, and how can they be improved to create more engagement? Don't hinder yourself with outdated traditions; keep them, modify them to improve them, and increase engagement through those essential traditions. Student voice matters. In fact, student voice matters so much that you should rely on it for specific feedback on what would help make your school environment exciting for your staff and students.

## Harnessing the Power of Music to Set the Tone

Music possesses a unique ability to shape the atmosphere and mood in various settings. One research study (Thoma et al., 2013) found that background music can influence the pace of activities. Fast-paced music leads to quicker eating, while softer, smoother tunes promote a calm environment. Whether it's a party with friends or a staff meeting after a long day, music has a neurological impact that naturally uplifts moods, making it a valuable tool to tap into whenever possible (Thoma et al., 2013).

In a school known for its best practices, music is integrated with student voice to foster a vibrant and engaging school atmosphere. Interactive iPads with feedback surveys are strategically placed in a prominent location outside the cafeteria, where students walk by daily. This setup allows students to suggest playlists and contribute to the musical ambiance during Friday passing periods. The transformation is remarkable; at times, you will hear students breaking out in song, joyfully singing along to their favorite tunes. The school radiates positivity, leaving students and staff in a great mood.

Guiding Questions:
1. How can music be used in educational settings to foster a positive and engaging environment for students and staff?
2. What are some creative ways of using the tools you already possess to involve students in selecting and curating music playlists for the school?

*Music in Staff Meetings and Professional Development Days* Music can change the tone of staff meetings and professional development days, particularly after long and tiring days. The atmosphere can be transformed by selecting music that resonates with the teaching staff, positively impacting conversations and interactions (Thoma et al., 2013). During introductions of new staff members at the beginning of the school year, incorporate their chosen walk-up songs, which creates an immediate and fun connection, allowing personalities to shine through.

Guiding Questions:

1. How can music be utilized in staff meetings and professional development days to improve educators' overall mood and engagement? What benefits can be gained by incorporating staff members' favorite music during team-building or introductory activities?

**Music in Sports and Competitive Environments** The influence of music in sports is undeniable, as it sets the tone for athletes and spectators alike. Music has been used to create a positive environment in locker rooms, on practice fields, and during games. At sporting events, dedicated audio support and music selection during critical moments can provide a psychological advantage, leveraging momentum and enhancing the overall experience. Recognizing that extracurricular activities are something students eagerly look forward to and can significantly contribute to keeping them engaged at school, these events need to be just as upbeat and exciting. When students willingly attend such events, it becomes a win, directly impacting school engagement and attendance.

Guiding Questions:

1. How can music effectively boost team morale and motivation in sports settings?
2. In what ways can music enhance the spectator experience during sporting events?

**Music in the Classroom** Incorporating music into the classroom can have numerous benefits (Chamorro-Premuzic, 2022). From setting an exciting tone as students enter the class to helping maintain the pace during collaborative activities, music can foster enthusiasm and engagement. Using music as a timer or transitional signal can facilitate smoother transitions between activities and capture students' attention. When students are excited to come into your class because of the environment you create, they will behave appropriately, have a strong desire to be there and learn, and eagerly look forward to coming to class. Incorporating music into educational settings has shown benefits in learning and memory retention. Certain types of music, such as classical or instrumental tracks, can improve learning outcomes and aid in information recall.

Guiding Questions:
1. How can music be integrated into classroom routines to create a positive and dynamic learning environment?
2. What types of music are best suited for different classroom activities and learning moments?

**Personal Reflection on Music Use** Reflect on your experiences with music and consider how it benefits you in various aspects of life, from work to social interactions and personal development. One study (Chamorro-Premuzic, 2022) highlighted the positive impact of music on individuals' moods in various environments. Here are a few examples:

1. Stress reduction: Music reduces stress and promotes relaxation. Listening to soothing music can help lower heart rate and blood pressure.
2. Improved focus and productivity: Playing background music, particularly instrumental or ambient music, has enhanced focus and cognitive performance. It can create a pleasant atmosphere and improve concentration, making it beneficial in classrooms or workspaces.
3. Positive emotions: Music can evoke emotions and create a positive atmosphere. Upbeat and uplifting music can boost mood,

increase happiness, and develop a sense of well-being among individuals.
4. Social connection: Music has a unifying effect and can foster social bonds. In environments like restaurants or social gatherings, music can create a shared experience, encourage conversation, and enhance individual social interactions.

Guiding Questions:
1. How have you experienced the impact of music on your mood and environment in different settings?
2. How can you harness the power of music to enhance your well-being and your experiences with your team and/or at work?

## Overcoming Challenges: A Journey of Resilience and Hope

In school, I qualified for free meals because of our family's socio-economically disadvantaged status. Each week, I received a manilla folder from the front office with raffle-looking tickets that would give me lunch daily in the cafeteria. I was grateful because that meant that I could eat something during the day if I wanted. However, I didn't typically have money for extras during the week.

I continued to learn through my high school years how to survive tough circumstances independently. Because of life's early lessons, I was not worried or afraid of what the present or future held for me. As a 17-year-old senior in high school, I found myself living alone. I did whatever it took to make ends meet and graduate. I had hope for a future that did not include financial hardships. I wasn't sure how I would do it, but I had hope that I would figure it out, and hope is a powerful motivator.

During the last half of my high school senior year, my immediate family of four had split in various directions, and I was left to live on my own. My brother was off to college five states away, and my parents moved to Las Vegas, Nevada, to begin their new life. My dad worked construction, and Las Vegas was booming with new developments. I was street-smart and confident in my own abilities to survive, which garnered confidence in my mom, who allowed the circumstances to unfold the way they did, and she followed my dad to Las Vegas.

I maintained my schooling and extra-curricular activities, including the many duties as the school's student body president at a large comprehensive high school of over 3,200 students. I also cared for myself, the house, bills, food, and other necessities. I managed the financial side of things with instructions from my parents that if I needed money, I should sell off our acquired life's possessions inside the home and make it work. I took care of myself and did what was necessary to survive. By having weekend garage sales and selling off our life's possessions, I would make the money necessary to maintain the home, buy food, and other living expenses. Occasionally, I would have one of my family's teenage friends help me with weekend yard sales to sell everything. Challenges were the norm, some too hard and personal to include here. At times, it was rough, but I knew that my hope for a better future would sustain me.

While at school, no one was any wiser about my situation and circumstances. At the time, I could have easily slipped through the cracks and not gone to school or pursued any other postsecondary options like trade school, military service, or anything else that would have been professionally beneficial. Fortunately, I was lucky; I had a brother I looked up to and I followed him 1,650 miles from my home to attend college. I didn't even know what an SAT exam to get into college was until the college recruiter my brother told me to call explained it to me. I barely got into school. What would my future have been without my brother?

The question I pose to you is: What systems do schools have in place to ensure the readiness of all students for postsecondary endeavors, whether in a trade, college, or military venture? Is there a data wall in place to ensure that no one slips through the gaps, academically or emotionally?

## The Power of the Data Wall

Do you know where all your students stand academically? Do you have a comprehensive view of their academic journey, even tracing back to their early years? How do you ensure that no student falls through the cracks academically? How about their well-being? Data walls can help answer these and other questions. Our data walls were born from a desire for a living, interactive document that continuously evolves based on new data and student needs. The aim is to provide teachers, counselors, and administrators with a dynamic platform that offers deep insights into student performance and well-being.

At one school, the data wall is a repository of academic data that extends back to each student's 3rd-grade year of state assessment information. It incorporates various data points, including beginning, middle, and end-of-year data from core subjects such as math and reading. Additionally, campus and district-based assessments and universal screeners find their place on the data wall. Teachers and administrators actively engage with this data through regular reviews and frequent analysis. PLCs are conducted in the PLC room, which houses the data wall, so it is nearly a daily occurrence for educators to access the data wall.

The data wall becomes integral to our educational process, transforming how educators understand, support, and empower our students. It ensures that no student's academic journey goes unnoticed or unsupported, fostering a culture of data-driven excellence. Often, educational institutions focus solely on academic performance, neglecting the broader aspects of a student's life. Yet, on a comprehensive data wall, a student's personal well-being is closely interconnected with their educational journey.

The data wall is actively used by a team of educators, including counselors, assistant principals, and teachers. It serves as a centralized platform for collecting and analyzing data related to students' academic performance, social-emotional well-being, attendance records, and engagement levels. This data is not limited to grades and test scores but also includes information about students' social interactions and personal challenges. Also included in the data wall are student identifiers such as "At Risk," "Special Education," "Dyslexia Status," "Socio-Economically Disadvantaged," and more. These identifiers provide educators with essential information to better understand each student's needs and tailor their support accordingly. Naturally, the data wall is confidential and only viewable to educators with an educational interest in the information.

Ultimately, the information empowers educators to engage with the whole child through data, providing a holistic view of each student's academic journey. Moreover, the data wall ensures that data remains accessible over time, allowing educators to track historical and current trends and information about students, leading to more informed decision-making and tailored support.

The data wall allows educators to:

1. **Identify at-risk students:** Educators can pinpoint students struggling academically, emotionally, behaviorally, or socially. By recognizing early warning signs, they can provide timely and proactive intervention. This can improve student outcomes by giving educators valuable insights to prevent students from slipping through the cracks. In addition, patterns that may indicate a need for accommodations, such as special education or 504 support, become evident.

2. **Monitor progress:** The Data Wall enables educators to track each student's progress. This longitudinal view helps us assess the effectiveness of our interventions and adjust strategies accordingly for continuous improvement.

3. **Promote holistic development:** As a team, educators can address academic concerns and students' social and emotional well-being. This comprehensive approach ensures that we nurture the whole child, fostering a healthy and supportive school environment.

4. **Data-driven decision-making:** The team can make informed decisions based on concrete data rather than assumptions, leading to more effective strategies for improving student success.

5. **Improved engagement:** When students feel that their well-being is genuinely cared for, they are more likely to engage actively in their education. This, in turn, leads to better attendance and academic performance.

6. **Enhanced collaboration:** The data wall fosters collaboration among our leadership team members, including counselors, assistant principals, and teachers. This collaborative effort ensures that all aspects of student life are considered in their educational journey. The Data Wall fosters a Cross-Curricular collaborative approach among teachers. They continuously

discuss data, make informed decisions, and create strategies to support students across subjects.

7. **Small group interventions:** Data-driven insights lead to the creation of small groups for targeted interventions. Teachers can provide additional support to specific student groups based on their needs. In essence, the data wall is a powerful tool that helps us address the multifaceted needs of our students, fostering a positive and nurturing learning environment.

Additionally, the Data Wall integrates accountability and support systems within the school community. For instance, an attendance column allows the designated attendance overseer to flag students with frequent absences, ensuring that attendance issues are promptly addressed. This feature enhances the school's ability to support students' regular attendance.

The data wall promotes a sense of connectedness among students and educators. Educators can place their initials in a designated column next to the student's name if they have established a strong mentorship or trust-based connection with that student. This information proves invaluable, particularly when dealing with disciplinary matters. Assistant principals can refer to this data to identify the adults who may have a meaningful bond with the student, allowing for a more empathetic and effective approach to resolving issues.

Counselors also play a crucial role in utilizing the data wall. They can highlight a student's name when a significant life event may affect their academic performance and overall well-being. Whether it's a recent family loss, a divorce, or any other life-altering situation, counselors can provide the necessary support and resources to help these students navigate their challenges successfully.

Incorporating these elements into the data wall enhances its functionality and strengthens the school's support network. It creates a comprehensive system where accountability, mentorship, and social-emotional support converge, ultimately contributing to a more holistic and student-centric approach to education.

# CHAPTER 12

~

# Constructing an Elite Culture

Let's reflect on the essential objectives that will pave the way for a thriving educational environment and an elite culture. Our objectives served as the blueprint for constructing an Elite Culture's foundational pillars, focusing on High Standards and Positive Environment.

*Pillar 1: High Standards*
High Standards are the first pillar, representing a strong column of elite culture. Achieving this involves understanding and implementing the fundamental components of clear objectives towards your goals.

*Pillar 2: Positive Environment*
The second pillar, Positive Environment, forms the second main pillar upon which the Elite Culture stands. This is the desired environment in which individuals will thrive.

*Elite Mission*: Always clearly focus on the end goal, ensuring that every action aligns with the overarching mission.

*Elite Values*: The values upheld within the organization must be in harmony with the methods employed to accomplish the mission.

*Elite Strengths*: Recognizing and effectively using your unique personal strengths and talents, as well as those of others, is pivotal for maximizing potential and achieving success.

*Elite Team*: Assemble a team whose core values align with the mission, fostering a collaborative environment that propels the organization forward.

*Elite Awareness (Preventing Burnout and Retaining Talent)*: To retain talented individuals, it is crucial to develop a deep understanding of individual motivations, prevent burnout, and create a sense of connection.

*Elite Momentum*: Cultivate momentum by celebrating every achievement, irrespective of its scale, and foster collaboration, avoiding working in isolation.

*Elite Celebration*: Celebrate all victories to create a collective uplift that propels everyone's momentum forward.

*Elite Community*: Recruit families and engage the entire school or job community; building an Elite Culture truly takes a village.

*Elite Engagement*: Distinguish between engagement and compliance, emphasizing the importance of active involvement rather than mere adherence to established norms.

We've outlined the objectives and blueprint to guide you in creating and sustaining an Elite Culture with strong foundational pillars. By incorporating these key concepts into your particular setting, you're building an environment of excellence and fostering growth, collaboration, and a sense of purpose. May these objectives serve as your compass as you embark on the transformative journey of building an Elite Culture.

At the end of the day, craft your culture. Take control of what you can influence, leading with intentionality and dedication. One step at a time, one task at a time, one day at a time, you have the power to shape an environment of excellence. Those around you deserve it—and so do you!

# References

American Psychological Association (APA). (n.d.). [Online] Available at: https://www.apa.org/

The AVID institution website can be cited as follows:

AVID. (n.d.). AVID | Advancement Via Individual Determination. Retrieved from https://www.avid.org/

Brewer, Hamish. *Relentless.* Dave Burgess Consulting, Incorporated; First Edition (June 1, 2019).

Burgess, Dave. (2012). *Teach Like a Pirate*. Dave Burgess Consulting, Incorporated; Illustrated edition (August 18, 2012).

Casas, Jimmy. (2017). *Culturize*. Dave Burgess Consulting, INC.; Published in 2017.

Chapman, Gary. *The 5 Love Languages*. Northfield Publishing, 1992.

Chamorro-Premuzic, T. (2022) 'Can Music Make You More Productive?', Harvard Business Review, September 13. Available at: https://hbr.org/2022/09/can-music-make-you-more-productive

Chick-fil-A. (n.d.). How can I become a franchise Operator? Retrieved from https://www.chick-fil-a.com/customer-support/careers/working-at-a-chick-fil-a-restaurant/how-can-i-become-a-franchise-operator#:~:text=Generally%20speaking%2C%20we%20seek%20out,strive%20to%20be%20community%20leaders

Collins, Jim. Good to Great: Why Some Companies Make the Leap and Others Don't. HarperBusiness, 2001.

Gallup. "Employee Engagement Survey." Gallup, www.gallup.com.

Gallup, Inc. (2005). *Teach with Your Strengths*. Gallup Press; First Edition.

Gallup. (2015, October 8). Employees Who Use Their Strengths Outperform Those Who Don't. Retrieved from https://www.gallup.com/workplace/236561/employees-strengths-outperform-don.aspx

Gordon, Jon. (2018). *The Power of a Positive Team: Proven Principles and Practices that Make Great Teams Great*. Wiley; 1st edition (June 13, 2018).

Gordon, Jon. (2007). *The Energy Bus*. Wiley; 1st edition (January 22, 2007).

Gordon, Jon., & Van Allan, Jim. (2024). *The Energy Bus for Schools: 7 Ways to Improve Your School Culture, Remove Negativity, Energize Your Teachers, and Empower Your Students*. John Wiley & Sons Inc; Published on March 6, 2024.

Kagan, S., & Kagan, M. (2009). Kagan Cooperative Learning. San Clemente, CA: Kagan Publishing.

Lee, Julie. "Julie Lee, PhD - Director of Technology and Mental Health." Harvard Alumni for Mental Health, https://www.julieleephd.com/.

Maxwell, John C. (1998). *The 21 Irrefutable Laws of Leadership*. Thomas Nelson Inc.; Published in 1998.

Maxwell, John C. (2006). *The 360 Leader*. HarperChristian Resources.

National Association of Secondary Principals (NASSP). "NASSP Survey Signals a Looming Mass Exodus of Principals from Schools." December 8, 2021, www.nassp.org/news/nassp-survey-signals-a-looming-mass-exodus-of-principals-from-schools/.

National PTA. National Parent Teacher Association. [Online] Available at: https://www.pta.org/

Peale, Norman V. (1952). *The Power of Positive Thinking*. Prentice Hall.

Pep Unlimited LLC. (2022, September 23). Nick Saban Football HC, University of Alabama: Don't Worry about Winning. Just focus on Doing your Job at the Highest Level for Every Single Play and the Wins Will Follow. [Article].

Rath, Tom. (2007). *StrengthsFinder 2.0*. Gallup Press.

Saban, N. (2019, April 7). Press conference discussion on the five choices in life. [Transcript of press conference].

Sanfelippo, Joe. (2022). *Lead from Where You Are*. Impress, LP.

Texas Education Agency. (2022). 2022 School Report Card: Colleyville Middle (220906042). Retrieved from https://rptsvr1.tea.texas.gov/cgi/sas/broker?_service=marykay&_program=perfrept.perfmast.sas&_debug=0&ccyy=2022&lev=C&id=220906042&prgopt=reports%2Fsrc%2Fsrc.sas

Thoma MV, La Marca R, Brönnimann R, Finkel L, Ehlert U, Nater UM. The effect of music on the human stress response. PLoS One. 2013 Aug 5;8(8):e70156. doi: 10.1371/journal.pone.0070156. PMID: 23940541; PMCID: PMC3734071.

# Acknowledgments

I want to thank my wonderful family: Lacey, Gracey, and Ally. My three ladies have seen the behind-the-scenes work it takes to be a part of and also build various elite cultures. Also, to my mom, dad, and brother Danny. I wouldn't be where I am today without the unwavering support of my immediate and extended family.

In everything, I thank God for His grace as I am still a man in need of a savior daily.

To my friends, colleagues, and family who believed in me throughout life's journey.

I would like to express my sincere gratitude to everyone from the ConnectEDD Publishing team who provided me with the opportunity to publish this book, and to my friends who offered their invaluable insights to ensure its quality for the readers.

I'd like to express my heartfelt thanks to the educators who invest so much time in their students, coaches and fine arts teachers who extend beyond their extracurriculars, teaching invaluable life lessons and investing in the whole individual, preachers, and youth ministers who rooted me in my faith, and colleagues with whom I've shared the professional trenches united in a common purpose.

Finally, I thank everyone who took a chance on me and allowed me to have a seat at the leadership table.

# About the Author

Dr. David Arencibia is a highly regarded educator with over two decades of experience as a school leader, dedicated to building cultures of success. Some of David's notable accolades include being named the 2022 Texas Secondary Principal of the Year, the 2023 National Principal of the Year finalist, and the 2022 Texan of the Year finalist by the Dallas Morning News.

As principal, his school garnered recognition as one of the Best Schools in Texas and the United States, according to US News & World Report. Under his leadership, the school achieved significant milestones, earning designations such as being named a Nationally Recognized Model Campus, a Texas School To Watch, an "A" rated school, and a National PTA School of Excellence. Some notable achievements occurred during a school year when his school achieved

100% of the students experiencing at least a year's worth of academic growth, among other scores in Reading, Math, and Science that were the highest in school history for state testing.

Along with a group of colleagues, David has worked with the US Secretary of Education in Washington, D.C., several times, focusing on improving "Teacher Burnout" and "Overall Educational Improvement." He also worked with ESPN and the Choose Kindness Campaign in Los Angeles, California, during the College National Championship activities in collaboration with the Extra Yard for Teachers - College Football Playoff Foundation.

David is a sought-after Keynote Speaker who delivers professional development, leadership training, and workshops. He is also a certified Jon Gordon: *Energy Bus for Schools* Trainer and Speaker. In collaboration with best-selling author, speaker, and educational leader Jimmy Casas, David is also a part of the ConnectEDD Speaking Bureau.

Connect with David: For speaking engagements, workshops, professional development sessions, educational needs, or leadership coaching, contact David at 972-559-0463 or email info@davidarencibia.com For more information, visit: www.davidarencibia.com

# More from ConnectEDD Publishing

Since 2015, ConnectEDD has worked to transform education by empowering educators to become better-equipped to teach, learn, and lead. What started as a small company designed to provide professional learning events for educators has grown to include a variety of services to help educators and administrators address essential challenges. ConnectEDD offers instructional and leadership coaching, professional development workshops focusing on a variety of educational topics, a roster of nationally recognized educator associates who possess hands-on knowledge and experience, educational conferences custom-designed to meet the specific needs of schools, districts, and state/national organizations, and ongoing, personalized support, both virtually and onsite. In 2020, ConnectEDD expanded to include publishing services designed to provide busy educators with books and resources consisting of practical information on a wide variety of teaching, learning, and leadership topics. Please visit us online at connecteddpublishing.com or contact us at: info@connecteddpublishing.com

## Recent Publications:

*Live Your Excellence: Action Guide* by Jimmy Casas

*Culturize: Action Guide* by Jimmy Casas

*Daily Inspiration for Educators: Positive Thoughts for Every Day of the Year* by Jimmy Casas

*Eyes on Culture: Multiply Excellence in Your School* by Emily Paschall

*Pause. Breathe. Flourish. Living Your Best Life as an Educator* by William D. Parker

*L.E.A.R.N.E.R. Finding the True, Good, and Beautiful in Education* by Marita Diffenbaugh

*Educator Reflection Tips Volume II: Refining Our Practice* by Jami Fowler-White

*Handle With Care: Managing Difficult Situations in Schools with Dignity and Respect* by Jimmy Casas and Joy Kelly

*Disruptive Thinking: Preparing Learners for Their Future* by Eric Sheninger

*Permission to be Great: Increasing Engagement in Your School* by Dan Butler

*Daily Inspiration for Educators: Positive Thoughts for Every Day of the Year, Volume II* by Jimmy Casas

*The 6 Literacy Levers: Creating a Community of Readers* by Brad Gustafson

*The Educator's ATLAS: Your Roadmap to Engagement* by Weston Kieschnick

*In This Season: Words for the Heart* by Todd Nesloney, LaNesha Tabb, Tanner Olson, and Alice Lee

*Leading with a Humble Heart: A 40-Day Devotional for Leaders* by Zac Bauermaster

*Recalibrate the Culture: Our Why…Our Work…Our Values* by Jimmy Casas

*Creating Curious Classrooms: The Beauty of Questions* by Emma Chiappetta

*Crafting the Culture: 45 Reflections on What Matters Most* by Joe Sanfelippo and Jeffrey Zoul

*Improving School Mental Health: The Thriving School Community Solution* by Charle Peck and Dr. Cameron Caswell

*Building Authenticity: A Blueprint for the Leader Inside You* by Todd Nesloney and Tyler Cook

*Connecting Through Conversation: A Playbook for Talking with Kids* by Erika Bare and Tiffany Burns

*The Dream Factory: Designing a Purposeful Life* by Mark Trumbo

*Stories Behind Stances: Creating Empathy Through Hearing "The Other Side"* by Chris Singleton

*Happy Eyes: All Things to All People* by Ryan Tillman

*The Generative Age Artificial Intelligence and the Future of Education* by Alana Winnick

*Recalibrate the Culture: Action Guide* by Jimmy Casas

*Leading with PEOPLE: A Six Pillar Framework for Fruitful Leadership* by Zac Bauermaster

*A School Leader's Guide to Reclaiming Purpose* by Frederick C. Buskey

# ConnectEDD
## PUBLISHING

www.ingramcontent.com/pod-product-compliance
Lightning Source LLC
Chambersburg PA
CBHW070112030426

42335CB00016B/2124